WHAT REALLY HAPPENED IN NANKING

THE REFUTATION OF A COMMON MYTH

by **Tanaka Masaaki**
Translated by Sekai Shuppan

Sekai Shuppan, Inc., Tokyo

Published by Sekai Shuppan, Inc.
Shin Sakuma Big., 3F
2-13-14, Nishi-Shimbashi,
Minato-ku, Tokyo, 105-0003
Japan

Original Japanese language edition
published by Kenkosha, Tokyo, Japan, 1987.

Cover design by Hidaka Miki.

Printed in Japan.

ISBN 4-916079-07-8

TABLE OF CONTENTS

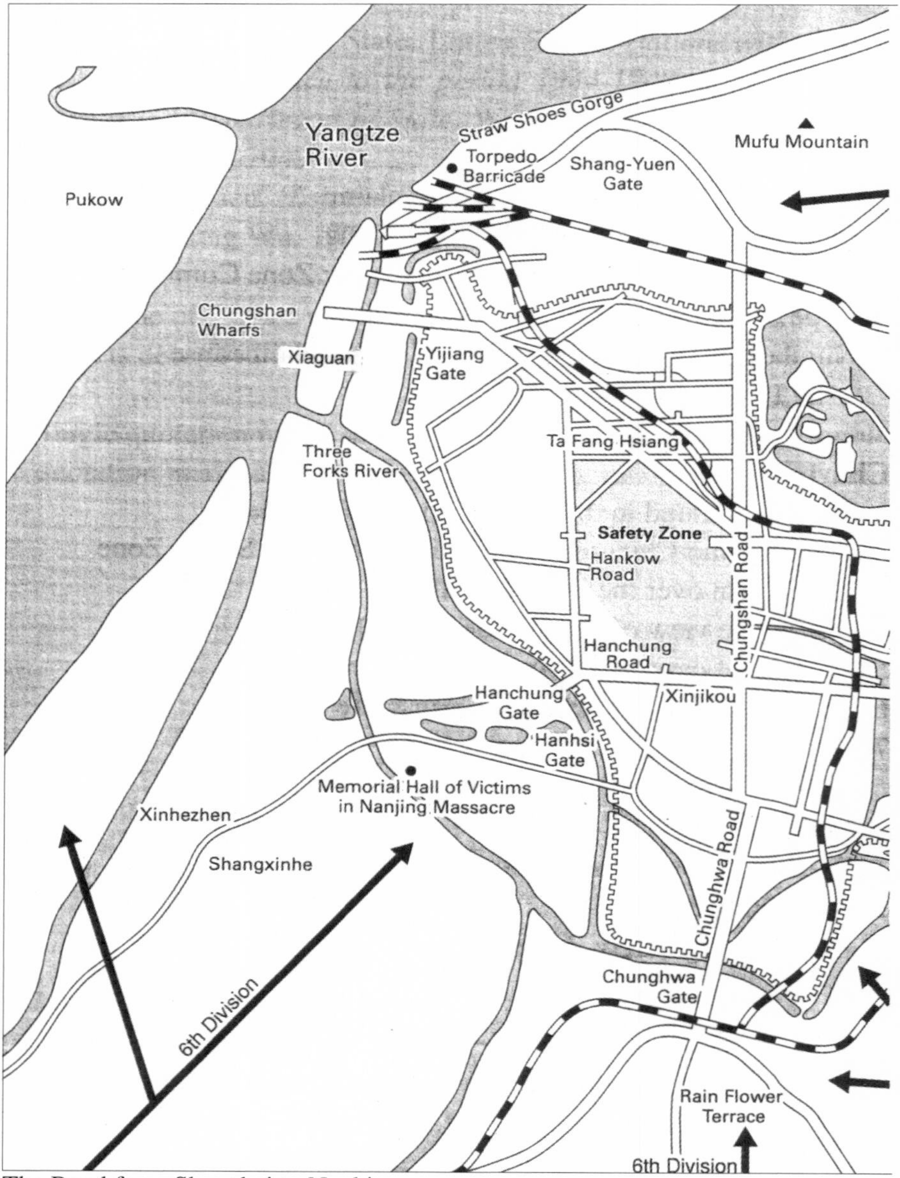

The Road from Shanghai to Nanking

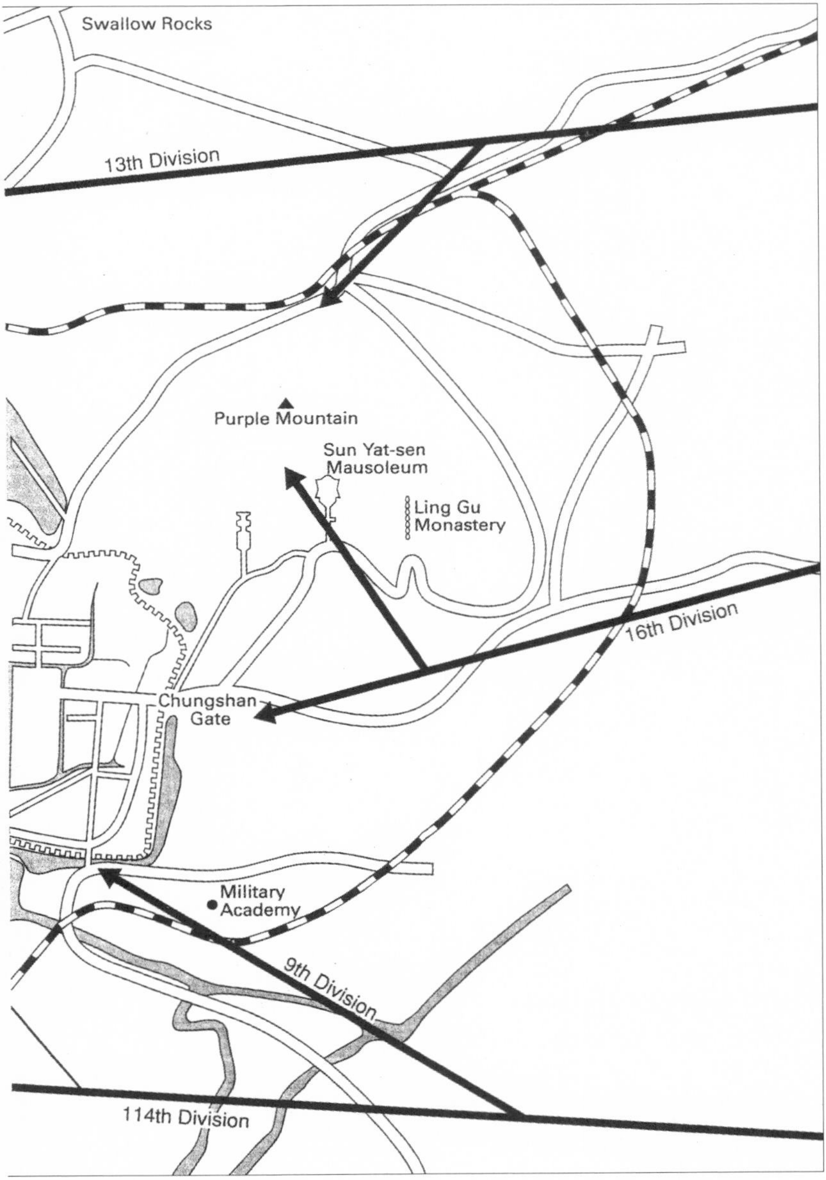

Swallow Rocks
13th Division
Purple Mountain
Sun Yat-sen Mausoleum
Ling Gu Monastery
16th Division
Chungshan Gate
Military Academy
9th Division
114th Division

Translator's Note

Japanese personal names have been rendered surname first, in accordance with Japanese custom.

The *hanyu pinyin* romanization system has been used to transliterate Chinese personal and place names, with the exception of Wade-Giles transliterations that are still in common use (e.g., Yangtze River, Chiang Kai-shek).

Foreword

The word *history* possesses two meanings. One is "events of the past in and of themselves." The other is "a record of events of the past put into writing for the benefit of future generations" (historiography). Before writing was invented, history was transmitted orally (and still is today in communities lacking a writing system). Once writing was invented and literacy became widespread, the oral tradition gave way to written records, the literature of history. Today, when we speak of history, we are usually referring to historiography, i.e., historical literature — the events of the past as expressed in writing.

Our perception of history derives from past events as transmitted via the written word, not from the events themselves. Is it possible for us to obtain an accurate understanding of past events? This is, epistemologically, a difficult question to answer. However, we must avoid the pitfalls of agnosticism, which is both nihilistic and unproductive, and resign ourselves to our fate as mere mortals: We cannot aspire to a totally accurate comprehension of historical facts through the medium of the written word, but we can arrive at an understanding that is a very close approximation.

Historical researchers must be aware of these possibilities (and limitations) before they embark on this intellectual activity. However, the transformation of the events of the past into the written word must always be guided by a conscientious effort to represent those events as authentically as possible. All historiographers who commit the fruits of their research to paper shoulder a weighty ethical responsibility, which involves selecting their words, the medium of facts, with the utmost care.

Unfortunately, those who engage in the recounting of history, a most sacred undertaking, do not always take this responsibility seriously. Some "historiographers" make no effort to choose words that most closely resemble the truth. Worse, they approach the task of writing history with the attitude that their use of forceful language will convince readers that they are conveying information that very closely resembles historical fact. They are unqualified to practice the art of historiography precisely because they do not have the requisite respect for the reasoning process (*logos*), on which their words should rightly be based. Nevertheless, we are confronted with many such charlatans who invent or intentionally misrepresent history and, regrettably, there is little we can do to stop them.

During the modern era, inventors of history found the perfect arena for their misdeeds — the IMTFE (International Military Tribune for the Far East, commonly known as the "Tokyo Trials"), held between 1946 and 1948 in Japan's capital, Tokyo. For their main theme, they selected the Nanking Incident. Out of the occupation of the Nationalist Chinese capital by the Japanese military, which occurred during the course of a war, and which was otherwise unremarkable, they manufactured the "Nanking Massacre." Their handiwork soon gave rise to the illusion that their invention was fact. The illusion continued to gain force, until it became entrenched in the literature of history, as fact. The creation of the "Nanking Massacre" can be attributed to the Allied nations that prosecuted "war criminals" at the Tokyo Trials, and to the Republic of China which, lacking the conscience that inspires respect for the words of men, entered into a conspiracy with the witnesses it dispatched to the tribunal, where they lied on the witness stand.

From the opening of the Tokyo Trials in 1946 until April 1952, when the Treaty of Peace was signed in San Francisco and the sovereignty of Japan was restored, the citizens of Japan, an occupied nation, were unable to denounce or protest the fabrication of history perpetrated at the tribunal. Wrested of freedom of speech, they were powerless to object to the shower of baseless slanders and charges of nonexistent war crimes that fell upon them. During the Occupation, which spanned nearly seven years, the sins committed by the Japanese military in Nanking, products of their inventors' imaginations, were persistently and repeatedly broadcast throughout the world. This propaganda was spectacularly successful; it was embraced as fact by the international community, and engendered an inexorable, undeserved prejudice.

In April 1952, with freedom of speech finally restored to them, Japanese scholars debated the Nanking Incident, and exposed it for what it was — the falsest of falsehoods. They then attempted to share the information they had acquired in the hope of refuting the notion of a "Nanking Massacre." However, by that time, the aforementioned prejudice had become so widespread and so entrenched in the collective memory that it seemed impossible to dispel.

But once roused to action, Japan's scholars persevered. They were painfully aware of their responsibility toward the written word, and could not sit by in silence while the minds of the people of the world were being clouded by vicious Chinese propaganda. The work of every scholar who joined in this quest is significant, and there are quite a few books that I would be happy to recommend to English-speaking readers, since they describe events as they actually took place.

Among them, I have singled out the writings of Tanaka Masaaki. They merit special mention, since Mr. Tanaka was the pioneer in the search for the truth about the Nanking Incident. He began work on his refutation of the "Nanking Massacre" while the Tokyo Trials were still in session. Once freedom of speech was restored, he began to write in earnest. Over a period of nearly 50 years, he has honed his arguments, subjecting his writings to constant reanalysis and revision. In *What Really Happened in Nanking*, his definitive work on the subject, Mr. Tanaka presents judiciously reasoned arguments. Furthermore, his respect for the virtue and power (*logos*) of words is obvious, as is his dedication to the historiographer's mission: to portray the events of history as accurately as is humanly possible.It is my fervent hope that English speakers throughout the world will put aside any preconceptions they may harbor, and afford this book the audience that it so richly deserves.

Kobori Keiichiro, Ph.D.
Professor, Meisei University
Professor emeritus, Tokyo University

Introduction

The recent emergence of a problem that has affected Japan-U.S. relations is a serious cause for concern. At the root of this problem are allegations made by Chinese-American writer Iris Chang in her book entitled *The Rape of Nanking* (published in the United States in 1997) and the anti-Japanese campaigns it has instigated. The book's subtitle, *The Forgotten Holocaust of World War II*, likens what Chang refers to as the "Nanking Massacre" to Nazi attempts to exterminate the Jews.

In the first place, Japan resolved not to discriminate against Jews in the "Outline of Measures Towards Jewish Peoples" (1938),[1] and ultimately saved a significant number of Jews from the Holocaust.[2] Chang's portrayal of Japan as a nation complicit in the Holocaust — any holocaust — betrays her ignorance (and temerity).

The inflammatory prose that characterizes *The Rape of Nanking* is rife with accusations that are simply untrue and descriptions of despicable, horrific crimes that were never committed. The photographs she includes (12 pages) are, without exception, fakes.

Nevertheless, this book has succeeded in engendering hatred of Japan and the Japanese in the hearts of Americans, though the great majority of them neither knew about nor were interested in the hostilities that took place in Nanking 63 years ago prior to its publication. Thanks to the energetic support and propagandizing of Chinese activist groups based in the United States, *The Rape of Nanking* quickly became a bestseller, with more than 500,000 copies sold to date. It has also created political tension between the two nations. For instance, in August 1999, the California State Assembly passed a resolution (AJR 27) urging Japan to apologize for wartime atrocities and to pay reparations to the victims of those atrocities.

How did the Japanese government respond to these insults? Saito Kunihiko, Japan's ambassador to the United States, agreed to enter into a televised dialogue with Chang. However, during the dialogue, he uttered not one word of protest against Chang's lies, hyperbole, and propaganda. Mr. Saito's only response was to state that Japanese history textbooks do indeed contain accounts of the Nanking Incident (until recently, this term was used to describe the battles that were waged in and around Nanking and the subsequent occupation — nothing more). The journalists who had comprised the studio audience then reported in the American media that the Japanese government had corroborated Chang's allegations, i.e., that the Japanese massacred 300,000 Chinese in Nanking, and they are now teaching their children about the massacre via accounts in textbooks.

Matsui Iwane was, without question, the most illustrious Japanese officer of his time. He graduated from the Military Staff College at the head of his class, for which achievement Emperor Showa presented him with a Japanese sword. Soon thereafter, Matsui was posted to China, where he remained for 16 years, and supported Sun Yatsen in his second revolution against Yuan Shikai. A staunch advocate of a united Asia, Matsui was the Army's China expert.

When fighting broke out between the Japanese and Chinese in Shanghai in 1937, the Headquarters of the General Staff dispatched the Shanghai Expeditionary Force and ordered Gen. Matsui into active service as its commander-in-chief. The Japanese had only 25,000 men at their disposal, while the Chinese had 300,000. Japanese military authorities, realizing that reinforcements were required, mobilized the 10th Army, commanded by Lt.-Gen.

Yanagawa Heisuke, which landed at Hangzhou on November 5. The Japanese emerged victorious. On December 1, Tada Hayao, Subchief of the General Staff, flew to Shanghai and issued the order to attack Nanking. The 10th Army and the Shanghai Expeditionary Force were combined to form the Central China Area Army, of which Gen. Matsui was appointed commander-in-chief.

The Central China Area Army then advanced to Nanking. Gen. Matsui issued a warning to Nanking Defense Corps commander-in-chief Tang Shengzhi, urging him to open the gates of the city and admit Japanese troops without offering any resistance, but the warning was rejected. On December 10, the Japanese decided to launch a massive assault on Nanking. Gen. Matsui gathered his subordinates and conveyed the following instructions: "The entrance of the Imperial Army into the capital of a foreign nation is an historic event. The attention of the world will be focused on you. You are to observe military regulations to the letter, to set an example for the future." He ensured that all his men received a map of Nanking and vicinity, with the Zhongshan Tomb (where Sun Yatsen is interred), the Ming Xiao Tomb, foreign legations, and other places where they were prohibited from entering clearly marked, and ordered sentries to be posted at each one of them. He added, "Anyone who loots or starts a fire, even accidentally, will be severely punished."

On December 13, Nanking fell to the Japanese. They made a ceremonial entry into the city on December 17, and on the following day, held a memorial service for the war dead. Concerned that no one would be praying for the repose of their souls, Gen. Matsui proposed that the Chinese war dead be honored at the same service. However, staff officers and division commanders objected; the service was held only for Japanese soldiers killed in action. (However, Japanese military authorities later conducted memorial services for fallen Chinese soldiers, on February 2 and 28, as described on p. 126,127) Even after Gen. Matsui returned to Japan, his sentiments did not change. In 1940, he erected a shrine dedicated to a united Asia in honor both the Japanese and Chinese war dead, on Mt. Izu in Atami.

According to an essay he wrote about the construction of the shrine, Gen. Matsui very much regretted having to wage war with a neighboring nation, especially one that he admired. However, he believed that the conflict would eventually go down in history as a righteous war that had ultimately rescued the peoples of East Asia from European domination and lay the foundation for their independence. Gen. Matsui prophesied that an Asian revival was imminent.

To soil that he had had shipped to Japan from the battlefields of Central China, stained with the blood of both Japanese and Chinese soldiers, Gen. Matsui added Japanese clay. He then commissioned master potter Shibayama Seifu to create a statue of Kannon, the goddess of mercy measuring 3.3 meters in height. He commissioned Kato Haruji, awarded Living National Treasure status by the Japanese government, to craft another statue of Kannon (60.6 cm high) for the main hall of the shrine. To the right of this statue, Gen. Matsui had a memorial tablet honoring Japanese soldiers killed in action, and to its left, an identical tablet for the Nationalist soldiers. Surplus lumber from the Atsuta Shrine in Nagoya was used to build the main hall. For the solemn consecration ceremony, the venerable priest Tessui was summoned from Tokyo. Would an officer as honorable and ethical as Gen. Matsui have ordered or sanctioned the massacre of 300,000 Chinese?

In March 1938, Gen. Matsui returned to Japan from Nanking. After reporting to the Emperor, he visited army hospitals in Osaka, Nagoya, Sendai and other parts of Japan, comforting his wounded or ailing subordinates. I accompanied him on these visits. At some point during our travels, he told me that he wondered whether Nanking was still a peaceful, orderly city, and asked me to go there to investigate.

In July 1938, seven months after the fall of Nanking, I inspected former battle sites at Yuhuatai, Zijinshan, Xiaguan, and Xinhezhen. Additionally, I explored every inch of Nanking. The population had already risen to nearly 400,000. Merchants were prospering, and the city was safe enough for women to venture out alone at night. I submitted a report to that effect to Gen. Matsui.

In 1942, at the age of 32, I was drafted into the Army. I was assigned to the Central China Field Ordnance Depot in Shanghai. I heard Emperor Showa's radio broadcast announcing the end of World War II at the Branch Ordnance Depot in Wuxi, in 1945. By the time I returned to my home in Nagano, it was April 1946.

I learned that Gen. Matsui had been charged with Class A war crimes, and had been incarcerated at Sugamo Prison in Tokyo. I travelled from Nagano three times to visit him. He told me that he had never heard a word about a massacre in Nanking until the Tokyo Trials began. He had left Nanking for Shanghai a week after the ceremonial entry into that city. At two press conferences he held for foreign journalists, no one mentioned a massacre.

Sixth Division commander Lt.-Gen. Tani Hisao, who was sentenced to death at a war crimes trial held in Nanking, said that he was astonished when he first heard about the "massacre." He hadn't heard anything about one from his subordinates or anyone else, for that matter.

When I heard that William Webb, the presiding justice at the Tokyo Trials, had sentenced Gen. Matsui, the man whom I respected more than anyone else on earth, to death by hanging, I was devastated — so much so that I couldn't eat. To console myself, and in the hope of spreading the truth to the widest audience possible, I began to write. My first book was *Justice Radhabinod Pal*[3] *Absolves Japan*.[4] Later, I produced four more books: *The Truth About the Tokyo Trials*,[5] *The Fabrication of the Nanking Massacre*,[6] *The War Journal of General Matsui Iwane*,[7] and *What Really Happened in Nanking: The Refutation of a Common Myth*.[8]

I believe that *What Really Happened in Nanking* is my representative work, the fruit of long years of research on this subject, and tells the true story of what happened in Nanking. The English-language version contains only part of the original book, but it covers all the main points made therein. I urge American researchers, politicians, scholars, journalists, and opinion leaders to read it. Once they have, I am convinced that they will arrive at the realization that violations of international law of the magnitude alleged by Iris Chang in *The Rape of Nanking* (more than 300,000 murders and 80,000 rapes) never took place.

This problem threatens not only Japan-U.S. relations, but also world peace. Both nations must be careful to avoid being misled by misinterpretations and demagoguery, and make an earnest effort to seek the truth.

In conclusion, I would like thank Professor Kobori Keiichiro for contributing the Foreword. To Mr. Moteki Hiromichi, president of Sekai Shuppan, Inc., I offer my deepest appreciation for his encouragement, and for shouldering the responsibility for all matters relating to the translation and publication of this book.

Statue of Koa Kannon on Mt. Izu, Atami

Chapter 1

Defining "Massacre"

Some refer to the hostilities that took place in Nanking in December 1937 and events that followed them as a massacre. Before we begin our examination of the "Nanking Massacre," we must first define the word massacre. Otherwise, we may repeat a mistake that others have made and view combatants who lost their lives as victims of a massacre. A major battle was fought in Nanking, and it claimed the lives of a large number of soldiers. The Battle of Iwo Jima, waged between Japanese and American forces, claimed many more lives (at least 27,000), but no one speaks of an "Iwo Jima Massacre."

Since international law does not define "massacre" *per se*, we shall construe the word as the unlawful, premeditated, methodical killing of large numbers of innocent people. We are saddened by the claims that Japanese military personnel were guilty of a massacre in Nanking, and that all who died during or as a result of the hostilities — be they soldiers who died in combat, stragglers killed during subsequent sweeps, or Chinese troops masquerading as civilians, who were apprehended and executed — were victims of a massacre. However, we are confident that anyone who reads this book will realize that nothing remotely resembling a massacre took place in Nanking.

At the IMTFE (International Military Tribune for the Far East, also known as the "Tokyo Trials"), the prosecution made various assertions as to the number of persons massacred in

Nanking: 127,000, 200,000, and 100,000.[9] In recent years, the original, postwar Chinese claim of 300,000 victims has escalated to 400,000.

Even among Japanese scholars, the number of "victims" varies considerably. Former Waseda University professor Hora Tomio, a historian and arguably the leading proponent of the "massacre" argument, believes there were 200,000 victims. Nihon University professor Hata Ikuhiko, who is viewed as a moderate in this controversy, has arrived at the figure of 40,000. Independent researchers Itakura Yoshiaki and Unemoto Masami, both of whom oppose the "massacre" theory, have posited 6,000-13,000 and 3,000-6,000, respectively. The bases for the various arguments (or the lack thereof) aside, the real problem that we face is the way in which persons who lost their lives during or after the conflict are classified: noncombatants, soldiers disguised as civilians, soldiers who surrendered, prisoners of war, and stragglers. Each category is different in nature. We believe that the following classification system used by Unemoto in *Eyewitness Accounts of the Battle of Nanking* is the most accurate.

Once the victims of the hostilities in Nanking have been properly classified, we discover that the majority of them died in combat or of combat-related causes. Far fewer deaths were the result of unlawful acts. It is true that Chinese soldiers who had surrendered were occasionally shot on the spot due to extenuating circumstances. And some civilians were killed accidentally during searches for soldiers who had donned civilian clothing and infiltrated the Safety Zone. (The Nationalist military authorities must bear the responsibility for civilian deaths, since they tolerated the presence of armed Chinese combatants in the Safety Zone, in violation of international law.) However regrettable, tragedies like these were an inevitable byproduct of war.

No contemporaneous account refers to the mass murder of innocent civilians in Nanking. We will discuss this subject in greater depth later on in this book. But we wish to emphasize that the issue at hand is the number of deaths attributable to unlawful acts.

It is our earnest hope that readers will be mindful of this distinction as they consider the arguments presented in this book.

Category	Cause of Death
Combat casualties	(1) Soldiers who died while defending Nanking (2) Soldiers who were shot to death while retreating or fleeing (3) Soldiers who were shot to death during the hunt for stragglers (4) Soldiers disguised as civilians who were apprehended and executed
Combat-related casualties	(1) Individual soldiers who surrendered and were later killed (2) Civilians who remained in the battle zone to aid Chinese troops, or who were caught up entangled in the hostilities and died as a result (3) Civilians who were killed accidentally during the hunt for soldiers masquerading as civilians
Unlawful acts	(1) Groups of prisoners of war or individual prisoners of war who were incarcerated and subsequently executed (2) Innocent civilians (including women and children) who were killed

Source: Unemoto Masami, "Shogen ni yoru Nankin senshi" (Eyewitness Accounts of the Battle of Nanking) (Tokyo: *Kaiko*, February 1985), Part 11.

Chapter 2

Population of Nanking in 1937

The first issue that must be addressed in any discussion of the Nanking Incident is: What was the population of Nanking when the Japanese attacked the city in December 1937?

On December 1, 1937, Ma Chaojun, the mayor of Nanking, ordered all residents to take refuge in a zone administered by the International Committee for the Nanking Safety Zone (referred to hereafter as the "International Committee.") After providing the Committee with a supply of rice and wheat, some currency, and a few police officers, Ma fled Nanking on the heels of Generalissimo Chiang Kai-shek and other Nationalist leaders. By that time, Nanking's wealthy and middle-class residents, as well as the city's government officials, had already fled to the upper reaches of the Yangtze. The majority of those remaining in Nanking were poor people, who lacked the means to travel elsewhere.

At that time, Nanking was the capital of China. The word "capital" usually conjures up an image of a huge city, but Nanking is far smaller than Kyoto, Beijing, or Shanghai. According to a 1937 map, the city measured five kilometers from east to west. It was possible to walk from the largest gate, Zhongshan Gate, to Hanzhong Gate in about an hour. From Zhonghua Gate at the south end of the city, one could walk the 11 kilometers to Yijiang Gate, at the north end, in less than two-and-a-half hours. Nanking

Number 7, Political and Economic Studies

南京安全區檔案

DOCUMENTS OF THE NANKING SAFETY ZONE

EDITED BY

SHUHSI HSÜ, PH.D.

Sometime Adviser to the Ministry of Foreign Affairs

徐淑希纂

Prepared under the Auspices of the Council of International Affairs, Chungking

KELLY & WALSH, LIMITED

SHANGHAI — HONG KONG — SINGAPORE

1939

A 167-page book containing 69 missives issued by the International Committee, and addressed to the Japanese, American, British, and German embassies. It is one of the most important contemporaneous sources on Nanking.

occupied an area of approximately 40 square kilometers (if one includes Xiaguan, which is outside the city limits), equivalent to 70% of Manhattan Island (57 square kilometers). Within its narrow confines were an airfield, low mountains, and farms.

The Safety Zone was established in an 3.8-square-kilometer area of Nanking, about the size of New York City's Central Park (3.40 square kilometers). It was administered by the members of the International Committee, all of whom were citizens of foreign nations. They gathered all the residents into the Safety Zone and endeavored to feed and house them. Between December 13 (the day the Japanese breached the gates of Nanking) and February 9, 1938, the International Committee issued 69 missives addressed and hand-delivered to the Japanese, American, British, and German embassies, on an almost daily basis. Most of them are complaints about misconduct on the part of Japanese military personnel, or pleas to military authorities to improve public safety or supply food to the refugees. These 69 documents are contemporaneous records, and should certainly be considered primary sources. Unfortunately, the Japanese Foreign Ministry burned them toward the end of World War II, so the Embassy's copies are no longer extant. But they were compiled by Dr. Hsü Shuhsi, a professor at Beijing University, under the title *Documents of the Nanking Safety Zone*. Many of them also appear in *What War Means*,[10] edited by *Manchester Guardian* correspondent Harold Timperley, and were submitted as evidence to the IMTFE. As shown in the photograph on p. 11, the version edited by Hsü Shuhsi bears the imprimatur of the Nationalist government: "Prepared under the auspices of the Council of International Affairs, Chunking." It was published by the Shanghai firm Kelly & Walsh in 1939. Any discourse on the Nanking Incident that disregards these valuable resources is suspect.

There are four references to the population of Nanking in late 1937 in *Documents of the Nanking Safety Zone*; all of them state that the total refugee population was 200,000.[11] A report written by James Espy, vice-consul at the American Embassy, and dispatched to the United States, and another report written by John

Rabe, chairman of the International Committee, also mention that Nanking's population was 200,000.

However, *Frankfurter Zeitung* correspondent Lily Abegg, who escaped from Nanking immediately before the city fell, wrote the following in an article dispatched from Hankou.

> Last week about 200,000 people left Nanking. One million souls once inhabited the city, but their numbers had dwindled to 350,000. Now there are at most 150,000 people remaining, but waves of evacuees seem interminable.[12]

Maj. Zhang Qunsi, who was taken prisoner by the Japanese, revealed that there were 50,000 Nanking Defense Corps soldiers and 100,000 noncombatants in the city. Another prisoner, Maj.-Gen. Liu Qixiong, who was later appointed head of the Nanking Military Academy (during Wang Jingwei's administration), and who commanded the brigade that defended the Yuhuatai position, estimated the population of Nanking as "approximately 200,000." In an entry in his war journal dated December 20, Gen. Matsui Iwane, commander-in-chief of the Shanghai Expeditionary Force wrote, "There are 120,000 Chinese in the Refugee Zone, most of them poor people."[13]

Taking all these sources into account, we can state with certainty that the population of Nanking at the end of 1937 was somewhere between 120,000 and 200,000. We know from contemporaneous records that the members of the Nanking Defense Corps, under the command of Tang Shengzhi, numbered between 35,000 and 50,000. Even allowing for gross underestimates, the population of Nanking could not have been less than 160,000 or more than 250,000. And even if the Japanese had murdered every single member of the Nanking Defense Corps and every single civilian, they could not have killed more than 160,000-250,000 Chinese. To massacre 300,000 persons, they would have had to kill many of them twice.

When confronted with these figures, proponents of the

massacre theory attempt to enlarge the civilian population of Nanking. For instance, Hora Tomio writes:

> When the Japanese military commenced its attack on Nanking, there were *reportedly* between 250,000 and 300,000 residents remaining in the city.
>
> *Reports* have it that after stragglers were eliminated during the sweep, there were nearly 200,000 persons residing in Nanking.
>
> Therefore, by the process of subtraction, we arrive at a total of 50,000-100,000 massacre victims.[14] [Italics supplied.]

His repeated use of phrasing like "reportedly" and "reports have it" implies that his sources are, at best, rumors. Rumors do not constitute proof. Hora is simply allowing his imagination to run away with itself, or guessing. None of his claims is the least bit reliable.

Like Hora, the authors of *Testimonies: The Great Nanking Massacre* have inflated the population of Nanking to support their accusation that 300,000-400,000 persons were massacred.

> According to our research, the population of the Safety Zone, at its highest, was 290,000. When the massacre was nearing an end, and the enemy was forcing the refugees to leave the Safety Zone, it claimed that the population was 250,000. Therefore, the population had decreased by 40,000 in less than two months. There were many reasons for that decrease, but the primary reason was, without a doubt, the enemy's massacre of huge numbers of refugees.[15]

How did the authors arrive at the figure of 290,000? Like Hora, they present no proof. Iris Chang has inflated the population even further.

> If half of the population of Nanking fled into the Safety Zone during the worst of the massacre, then the other half — almost

> everyone who did not make it to the zone — probably died at the hands of the Japanese.[16]

In a letter to the Japanese Embassy dated December 17, 1937, John Rabe, chairman of the International Committee, wrote: "On the 13th when your troops entered the city, we had nearly all the civilian population gathered in a Zone."[17] Chang either disregarded this document or failed to consult it. Whatever the case, she has invented a group of people residing outside the Safety Zone, and numbering 200,000-300,000.

At the IMTFE, defense attorney Levin broached a question that pierced the heart of this problem.

> Mr. Brooks calls my attention to the fact that in another portion of the affidavit is contained the statement that 300,000 were killed in Nanking, and as I understand it the total population of Nanking is only 200,000.

Flustered, William Webb, the presiding justice, replied, "Well, you may have evidence of that, but you cannot get it in at this stage," thus suppressing any further discussion of the matter.[18]

Therefore, the question of the actual population of Nanking was never addressed at the IMTFE, and a most bizarre judgements was handed down, in which the (unsubstantiated) number of massacre victims was stated variously as 100,000, 200,000, 127,000, etc. Since then, proponents of the massacre have avoided the population issue, resorted to guesswork (Hora), or invented their own statistics, as Iris Chang did.

Chapter 3

Nanking's Population Swells as Residents Return

A decline in the population of Nanking following the hostilities would lend support to assertions that Japanese troops perpetrated a massacre there. However, the population did not decline — it swelled.

We refer readers to the table accompanying this chapter, which we have compiled from population statistics appearing in *Documents of the Nanking Safety Zone* and in the diaries of John Rabe, chairman of the International Committee. *Documents of the Nanking Safety Zone* is a primary source consisting of 69 missives sent by the International Committee for the Nanking Safety Zone to the Japanese Embassy and the embassies of the United States, Great Britain, and Germany. The International Committee undertook the task of feeding the refugees in the Safety Zone and, therefore, its members required an accurate grasp of the population.

Documents dated December 17, 18, 21, and 27 state that there were 200,000 refugees in Nanking. However, by January 14, the population had burgeoned to 250,000, where it remained until the end of February. Most of the increase can be accounted for by returning residents, who had fled to outlying areas to escape the war.

When the word spread that order had been restored to Nanking, streams of people entered the city and began preparations for the New Year holiday. According to the prosecution's general

POPULATION SHIFTS IN THE NANKING SAFETY ZONE

year	month date	Source		
		War Damage in the Nanking Area	*Documents of the Nanking Safety Zone*	*The Good Man of Nanking: The Diaries of John Rabe*
1937	November 25			200,000+ p. 62
	November 28			200,000 p. 62
	December 10			200,000 p. 94
	December 17		200,000 p. 17	
	December 18		200,000 p. 18, 20	
	December 21		200,000 p. 48	
	December 25			200,000 p. 143
	December 27		200,000 p. 57	
1938	January 14		250,000-300,000 p. 84	200,000 p. 184
	January 17		250,000 p. 87	250,000 p. 190
	January 18		250,000 p. 90	
	January 19		250,000 p. 90	
	January 22		250,000 p. 95	
	January 28		250,000 p. 112	
	February 10		250,000 p. 164	
	March	250,000-270,000 Table 1		

summation at the IMTFE, "Once the Japanese soldiers had obtained complete command of the city, an orgy of rape, murder, torture and pillage broke out and continued for six weeks."[19] This was an outright lie. Who would be foolish enough to return to a city where a massacre and unspeakable atrocities were taking place?

From late December through early January, Japanese troops issued 160,000 civilian passports to refugees in the Safety Zone during their attempts to ferret out Chinese soldiers masquerading as civilians. However, no passports were given to children under 10 or to the elderly (those aged 60 years and over). In a letter to Fukuda Tokuyasu of the Japanese Embassy, International Committee Chairman John Rabe wrote:

> We understand that you registered 160,000 people without including children under 10 years of age, and in some sections without including older women. Therefore there are probably 250,000 to 300,000 civilians in the city.[20]

At the end of March 1938, Lewis Smythe conducted his own census, hiring students to do the fieldwork. In a report entitled *War Damage in the Nanking Area*, he writes:

> We venture an estimate of 250,000 to 270,000 in late March, some of whom were inaccessible to the investigators, and some of whom were passed by; 221,000 are represented in the survey.[21]

Later on in the same document, Smythe refers to the population as of late May.

> On May 31, the residents gathered in the five district offices of the municipal government (including Hsiakwan [Xiaguan], but apparently no other actions outside the gates) numbered 277,000.[22]

He also mentions that "a noticeable inflow from less orderly areas near the city probably built up a small surplus over departures ... ."[23]

The population increase alone is proof that peace had been restored to Nanking.

In his war journal, Gen. Matsui wrote, "residents seem to be returning gradually."[24] But according to Chinese accounts, some of them presented at the IMFTE, the "massacre" reached its peak precisely one week after the Japanese occupation, when bands of Japanese soldiers shot every Chinese who crossed their paths, raped every woman they encountered, looted, and burned. Corpses were everywhere, mountains of them. Rivers of blood ran down the streets. If those accounts are accurate, why did so many residents return to a city that had been transformed to a hell on earth?

In an interview, Nishizaka Ataru, a former member of the 36th Infantry Regiment (the first unit to enter Nanking through Guanghua Gate), told this writer that his unit was ordered to march to Shanghai. While travelling east on Jurong Road on December 23, Nishizaka encountered many groups of refugees on their way back to Nanking.

The December 20, 1938 morning edition of the *Asahi Shinbun* devoted a half-page to a collection of photographs entitled "Peace Returns to Nanking," one of which was taken on December 18. Captioned "A group of returning refugees escorted by the Imperial Army" (see p. 118,119), it shows a group of 200-300 refugees lined up waiting to reenter Nanking. Would they have been so anxious to return during, or even after, a massacre?

Chapter 4

"Mountains of Dead Bodeis" That No One Saw

When he took the witness stand at the IMTFE, Red Swastika Society Vice-Chairman Xu Chuanyin testified as follows.

> The Japanese soldiers, when they entered the city — they were very very rough, and they were very barbarious: They shoot at everyone in sight. Anybody who runs away, or on the street, or hanging around somewhere, or peeking through the door, they shoot them — instant death.
>
> ...
>
> I saw the dead bodies lying everywhere, and some of the bodies are very badly mutilated. Some of dead bodies are lying there as they were, shot or killed, some kneeling, some bending, some on their sides, and some just with their legs and arms wide open. It shows that these been done by the Japanese, and I saw several Japanese were doing that at that very moment.
>
> One main street I even started try to count the number of corpses lying on both sides of the street, and I started to counting more than five hundred myself. I say it was no use counting them; I can never do that.[25]

Jinling University Professor Miner Searle Bates, an American, also testified at the IMTFE.

> The bodies of civilians lay on the streets and alleys in the vicinity of my own house for many days after the Japanese entry.
>
> ...
>
> Professor Smythe and I concluded, as a result of our investigations and observations and checking of burials, that twelve thousand civilians, men, women and children, were killed inside the walls within our own sure knowledge.[26]

Witness after witness described gruesome sights that they had seen in Nanking. There were "mountains of dead bodies" inside the city walls. Corpses filled not only Nanking's main roads, but also its lanes and alleys. "Knee-high rivers of blood flowed down the city's streets." "Bodies were piled up on the streets, and automobiles drove over them." The Japanese shrank in horror as they listened to and read about these ghastly testimonies for days on end. Every evening NHK Radio broadcast a program entitled "This Is the Truth," which recounted inhumane, barbaric acts perpetrated by Japanese military personnel in the most lurid, sensational manner. Japan's newspapers emulated this style in their coverage. But not one of the tens of thousands of soldiers and some 150 newspaper correspondents and photographers who followed them into Nanking ever saw anything of the sort.

On December 15, 1937, two days after the Japanese occupied Nanking, *Tokyo Nichinichi Shinbun* correspondents Wakaume and Murakami interviewed Bates at his home on the Jinling University campus. The professor greeted his two visitors jovially, shook hands with them, and told them that he was grateful to Japanese troops for their orderly entry into Nanking, and for having restored peace so expeditiously.[27] Why Bates later made an about-face and testified that "the bodies of civilians lay on the streets and alleys in the vicinity of my own house for many days after the Japanese entry" and that “twelve thousand civilians, men, women and children, were killed inside the walls” at the IMTFE we will never know. The reports Wakaume and Murakami dispatched to Japan mentioned nothing resembling Bates’ testimony. If, as Bates asserted, there were indeed 12,000 corpses strewn about a city the size of Manhattan Island, they would have filled every street, lane, and alley. The stench of decomposing bodies, which can be detected within 100 meters, would have pervaded the city, nauseating its residents. It would have permeated their clothing and lingered through several launderings. Even when the corpses had been removed, the foul odor would have persisted for three or four days.

Sakamoto Chikashi, commander of the 2nd Battalion, 23rd Infantry Regiment (from Miyakonojo, Miyazaki Prefecture), vividly recalls the situation in Nanking in December 1937.

> At about 8:00 a.m. on December 13, we commenced our operation. Having climbed over a section of a wall that had been breached, we assembled near the southwest corner of the city by about 10:30 a.m. ... The main strength of the Regiment advanced, moving along the city walls, looking for Chinese stragglers. My battalion headed north toward the eastern sector of Nanking. At about noon, I noticed a restaurant on the left side of the road. It was open for business, and we saw a man who appeared to be the owner inside. Accompanied by some of my men, I went in. We enjoyed our first decent meal in a long time. The owner was delighted when we paid him with silver coins.
> After resting for a bit, we marched on. At about 2:30 p.m., we arrived at Qingliangshan [also known as Wutaishan], where we confiscated six heavy guns. We received orders to halt our advance, and bivouacked in the vicinity that night.
>
> We didn’t inspect every single home, but other than the restaurant owner, we saw no civilians, no enemy soldiers, no dead bodies. Nor did we hear any significant gunfire.

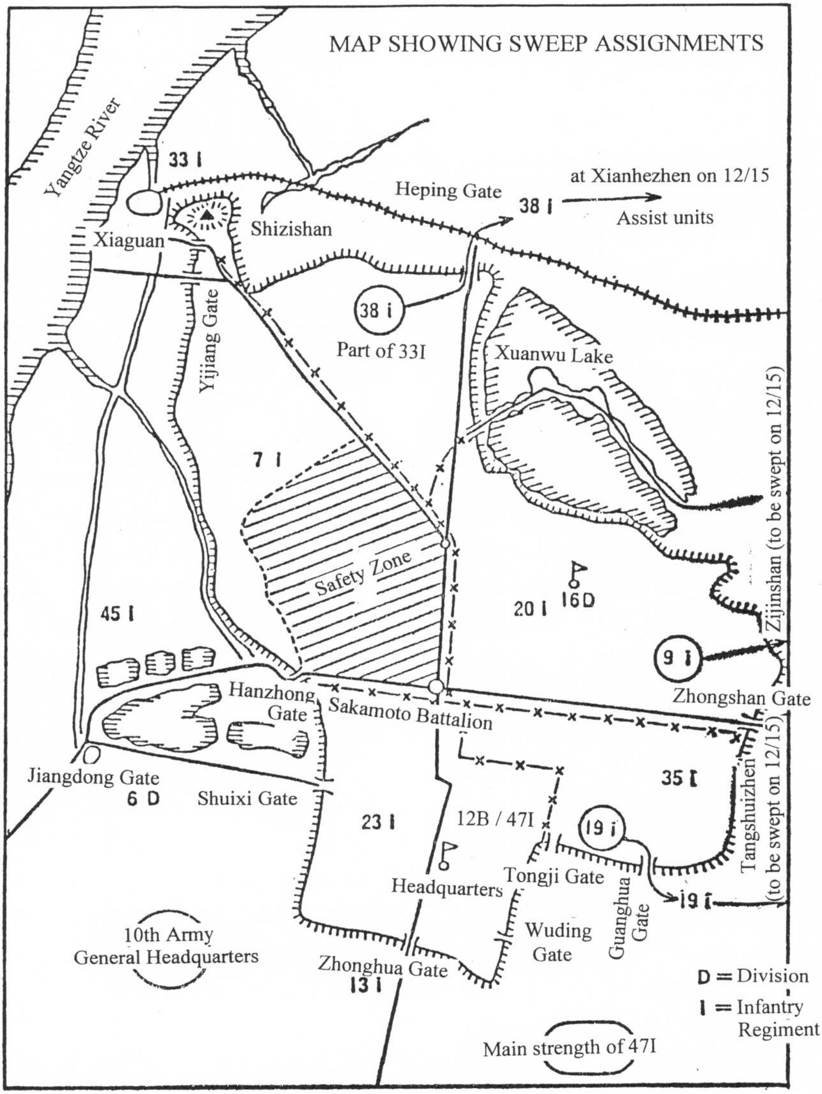
MAP SHOWING SWEEP ASSIGNMENTS
Yangtze River
33 I
Xiaguan
Shizishan
Heping Gate
38 I
at Xianhezhen on 12/15
Assist units
Yijiang Gate
38 i
Part of 33I
Xuanwu Lake
7 I
Safety Zone
20 I
16D
45 I
9 I
Zijinshan (to be swept on 12/15)
Hanzhong Gate
Sakamoto Battalion
Zhongshan Gate
Jiangdong Gate
6 D
Shuixi Gate
35 I
23 I
12B / 47I
19 i
Tangshuizhen (to be swept on 12/15)
Headquarters
Tongji Gate
19 I
Guanghua Gate
Wuding Gate
10th Army
General Headquarters
Zhonghua Gate
13 I
D = Division
I = Infantry Regiment
Main strength of 47I

> According to an article in the *Asahi Shinbun*, in *Travels in China*, Honda Katsuichi wrote that more than 20,000 Chinese were massacred at Wutaishan. However, as I mentioned earlier, all we did there was confiscate six guns. The same article also states that on December 13, Japanese troops blockaded the road to Xiaguan by closing Yijiang Gate, and shot a large number of fleeing civilians to death. At that time, we were in Qingliangshan. From there to Yijiang Gate, the distance is four or five kilometers as the crow flies. If something like that had happened, we would surely have heard the machine gun fire.[28]

At daybreak on December 13, Chinese troops began to retreat en masse. The Japanese entered Nanking from Zhongshan, Guanghua, Zhonghua, and Shuixi gates, and from Yijiang Gate at the northern end of the city. In the evening, each unit commenced its sweep of an assigned area (see map in p. 23). The sweep reached its peak on December 14 and was, for the most part, completed by December 15. The Japanese soldiers, who had anticipated fierce resistance, were astonished and unsettled by the silence that reigned in Nanking, and by the fact that they encountered no one there.

First Lt. Tsuchiya Shoji, commander of the 4th Company, 19th Infantry Regiment, entered Nanking through Guanghua Gate. His recollections of the events of December 13 follow.

> The walls had been destroyed by bombardment, but the homes inside were completely intact. Not even one roof tile had been displaced. However, an atmosphere of eerie silence and desolation pervaded the city, and even my stalwart subordinates hesitated for a moment. In the midst of this ineffable silence, one that I had never experienced before, I found myself, at some point, standing at the head of my company.
>
> As we proceeded further into the city, I sensed that Nanking was truly deserted. No enemy bullets flew at us. We saw no one — only endless, silent rows of houses. After we had advanced

> several kilometers (I don't remember how many) we came upon a huge, reinforced concrete building. We were not at all prepared for what we saw there.
>
> When we entered what seemed to be an auditorium, we saw many nurses tending to seriously wounded Chinese soldiers who couldn't be evacuated. The nurses just stood there and stared at us. I bowed to them, and left the building. We had resigned ourselves to a battle, but not a drop of blood was shed that day.[29]

Note that all these witnesses agree that Nanking was "eerily silent," orderly, and completely deserted.

The following is an excerpt from an interview this writer conducted with Tanida Isamu, former 10th Army staff officer.

> On the morning of December 14, Headquarters personnel entered Nanking. In the afternoon, we established a base in a bank building near Nanking Road. By that time, the city was already quiet. During the whole time I was stationed there, I heard no gunfire whatsoever. That same day, I made a tour of Nanking, and took photographs. I did see some corpses, but only a few. The city was peaceful.

As he spoke, Tanida showed me the photographs he had taken. He told me that he saw approximately 1,000 bodies at the wharf in Xiaguan, which he believed to be those of Chinese soldiers killed in action on December 13. I was amazed at the details he remembered. He also mentioned that December 14 is his birthday, and how pleased he was to have the opportunity to celebrate it in the company of Lt.-Gen. Yanagawa Heisuke, commander-in-chief of the 10th Army, and how they toasted each other with cold sake.

In *The Battle of Nanking*, Vol. 6,[30] former *Asahi Shinbun* correspondent Kondo states that "there were corpses of both Chinese and Japanese military personnel outside Guanghua Gate, the result of the bloody battle fought there. But I don't recall there being a lot of them. I saw no dead civilians." Also, Futamura Jiro, a photographer who worked for *Hochi Shinbun* and later *Mainichi Shinbun*, states, "Together with the 47th Infantry Regiment, I climbed over the wall into the city, but I saw very few corpses there."

We could cite any number of similar testimonies, but we believe that we have proved our point. No one saw "mountains of dead bodies" or "rivers of blood." No member of the Japanese military, no Japanese newspaper reporter, none of the 15 members of the International Committee, none of the five foreign reporters on assignment in Nanking, no foreign national saw scenes remotely resembling those described by Chinese witnesses who testified at the IMTFE.

Chapter 5

International Committee's Statistics on Crimes Attributed to Japanese Military Personnel

Among the 69 documents included in *Documents of the Nanking Safety Zone*, which describes the situation in Nanking following the Japanese occupation of that city, are reports of crimes allegedly committed by Japanese military personnel between December 13, 1937 and February 9, 1938. Any examination of these cases must be preceded by an awareness of the following facts.

1. All 15 members of the International Committee, which issued the reports, were foreign nationals (seven Americans, four Englishmen, three Germans, and one Dane). At the time, the nations they represented were, for all intents and purposes, Japan's enemies, in that they resented and opposed Japanese encroachments on Chinese territory and supported the Chinese military, both materially and spiritually. John Rabe, the Committee's chairman, was a citizen of Germany, a nation that was not friendly toward Japan, the popular perception notwithstanding. The German government supported the Chinese Nationalists, and supplied a team of military advisors headed by Gen. Alexander von Falkenhausen, which trained the Chinese Army. Rabe was president of Siemens' Far Eastern operations. During his assignment in China, he sold massive amounts of German-made weaponry to the Nationalist government.
2. Most of the crime reports prepared by Committee members were

based on hearsay or rumors (see table at the end of this chapter).

3. The Committee monitored crimes committed by Japanese troops both in the Safety Zone and in other parts of Nanking.
4. Serving as the Committee's informants were the Red Swastika Society, the YMCA, and a spy network of Chinese youths, a special detachment of the Nationalist government's Anti-Japanese Propaganda Bureau.[31]

As soon as the International Committee received information from these spy networks at its office at 5 Ninghai Road, one of its members would type up a report, which was then hand-delivered to the Japanese Embassy or other foreign legations. These reports were issued on a daily basis (in some cases, twice daily). In addition to letters accusing Japanese soldiers of crimes, the Japanese Embassy received requests for food and improved public safety. Additionally, several Committee members shared a residence, which served both as an information center where spies were received and as a conference site where demands and reports were drafted. Members made no attempt to investigate reports of Japanese crimes — they simply accepted all of them as fact and recorded them.

The Committee's liaison at the Japanese Embassy was Fukuda Tokuyasu. At the time, Fukuda was a junior foreign service officer. After his return to Japan, he was appointed private secretary to Prime Minister Yoshida Shigeru. He then embarked on a political career, serving first in Japan's Diet, and later as defense minister, director-general of the Administrative Management Agency, and then as posts and telecommunications minister. A gifted politician, Fukuda earned the respect and admiration of his compatriots. He was also a close friend of this writer, with whom he shared recollections of his service in Nanking.

> My duties included visiting the office of the International Committee, an organization formed by foreign nationals, nearly every day. There was much coming and going of Chinese youths, who were reporting incidents. Usually, what they had to say was

something like the following: "Japanese soldiers are gang-raping 15 or 16 girls on X Street right now" or "A band of Japanese soldiers has broken into a house on Taiping Street, and is now burglarizing it." Whichever Committee member or members was available (Rev. Magee, and Mr. Fitch, for instance) would proceed to type up the reports right in front of my eyes.

I voiced my objections to these reports any number of times: "Just a moment — you can't submit a protest without verifying this incident." Sometimes I would insist that Committee members accompany me to the site where the rape or looting had supposedly taken place. When we arrived there, we never found evidence of a crime's having been committed. None of these places was even occupied.

One morning, the embassy received a complaint from the American vice-consul: He had been told that Japanese soldiers were stealing lumber from an American-owned warehouse in Xiaguan and loading it onto a truck. I was ordered to go to Xiaguan immediately and stop them. I telephoned Headquarters and asked Staff Officer Hongo Tadao to accompany me there. Together with the vice-consul, we rushed to Xiaguan in the middle of a snowstorm. It must have been about 9:00 in the morning. When we arrived, there wasn't a soul there. The warehouse was locked. Nothing had been stolen. I scolded the vice-consul for making such a fuss over nothing. We received false alarms like that almost every day.

I am convinced that most of the reports that appear in Timperley's *Japanese Terror in China*[32] were typed by Fitch or Magee and sent to Shanghai without anyone's having inspected the alleged crime scene.

In the 69 letters written by the International Committee are accounts of 444 crimes allegedly perpetrated by Japanese military personnel. Accounts of only 398 cases were published in

Documents of the Nanking Safety Zone, most likely because Committee members had decided that the remaining 46 cases were particularly unconvincing.

In Nanking, Fukuda examined protests issued by Chinese citizens and the International Committee with care. He knew that most of them were completely without merit. Nevertheless, the stream of protests from the International Committee against Japanese acts of violence alarmed the East Asian Bureau of the Foreign Ministry. Ishii Itaro, then head of the Bureau, describes the reaction at the Ministry in his memoirs. The following excerpt is from a diary entry dated January 6, 1938.

> We received letters from Shanghai detailing unspeakable acts of violence, including looting and rapes, committed in Nanking by our soldiers. The perpetrators of these crimes have disgraced the Imperial Army and betrayed the Japanese people. This is a matter with grave social implications. ... How could men fighting in the name of our Emperor behave in such a way? From that time on, I referred to those incidents as the "Nanking atrocities."[33]

Japanese proponents of the massacre argument make liberal use of this passage, but they do so without a proper understanding of Ishii's reasons for believing the unfounded protests or of his animosity toward the military. At a liaison conference held at the Headquarters of the General Staff in Tokyo on December 14, 1938 (one day after the occupation of Nanking), an angry Ishii lashed out at military officials.

> At this point, who cares about the proposal [outlining conditions for peace]? Japan should go as far as it can go. When it reaches an impasse, it will be forced to see the light.[34]

> I experienced a perverse pleasure upon uttering those rebellious words.[35]

The "Nanking atrocities" had provided Ishii with the perfect opportunity to strike back at military authorities. His hatred of them may have stemmed from personal feelings of hostility toward his own nation. For instance, every time he mentions relations between Japan and China in his memoirs, he writes "China" first, contrary to the conventional method, an indication that his sympathies lay with China. Furthermore, when he was decorated by the Emperor, he wrote that he "wasn't at all pleased."[36] However, when he received a similar award from China, he expressed delight at having been so honored.[37] We find it ironic that a person harboring such sentiments was chief of the Foreign Ministry's East Asian Bureau.

We have digressed a bit, but we felt it was important to include this information, since Hitotsubashi University professor Fujiwara Akira, in his recent book,[38] cites Ishii's memoirs as irrefutable proof that a massacre was perpetrated in Nanking.

As Fukuda Tokuyasu has revealed, though the majority of the 398 "cases of disorder by Japanese soldiers in the Safety Zone" protested by the International Committee had no basis in fact, every one of them was accepted, documented, and reported to the Japanese Embassy. Tomizawa Shigenobu, an independent researcher, has made a computer analysis of these cases, which appears in table form at the end of this chapter.

There were 516 cases in all, not 398, since some of them include accounts of two incidents. Among them are 27 murder cases (54 victims). In only two cases are the names of the victims specified, and there were eyewitnesses to only one case. Two hundred thousand people were crowded into the Safety Zone, which encompassed an area the size of New York's Central Park but, incredibly, only one murder caught the attention of the Zone's residents. Since the International Committee accepted any and all rumors, 27 murder cases were recorded and protested, despite the absence of specifics or witnesses. Where did a massacre of *any* extent take place?

Thus were the accounts of all acts of misconduct occurring between December 13, 1937 and February 9, 1938, for which Japanese military personnel were allegedly responsible, documented by the International Committee, all of whose members harbored malice toward Japan.

STATISTICAL SUMMARY OF INCIDENTS REPORTED IN *DOCUMENTS OF THE NANKING SAFETY ZONE*

	Total number of incidents	Incidents occurring at night*	Incidents occurring during the day
Murders (Number of victims)	27 (54)	7 (12)	20 (42)
Rapes (Number of victims)	175 (375)	46 (187)	129 (188)
Abductions (Number of victims)	43 (370)	13 (34)	30 (336)
Looting	131	19	112
Arson	5	2	3
Bodily injury (Number of victims)	37 (43)	11 (15)	26 (28)
Trespassing	25	7	18
Others	73	16	57
TOTALS	516	121	395

Source: Tomizawa Shigenobu, *Nankin jiken no tokeiteki kenkyu* (Statistical Research on the Nanking Incident) (Tokyo, July 2000, photocopy).

* Japanese soldiers were not permitted to leave their barracks at night. Anyone who defied this order was severely punished. Furthermore, throughout the month of December, the electric power plant in Nanking was not functioning, so there was no electricity. At night, it was pitch dark in the city, and all who

Reports not signed by a Committee member	Reports signed by a Committee member	Reports that do not include victims' names	Reports that include victims' names	Cases for which there were eyewitnesses
6 (6)	14 (36)	12 (34)	2 (2)	1 (1)
75 (83)	54 (105)	51 (102)	3 (3)	7
5 (6)	25 (330)	18 (320)	7 (10)	2
57	55	8	47	5
2	1	0	1	0
10 (12)	16 (16)	14 (14)	2 (2)	0
6	12	0	12	7
44	13	5	8	4
205	190	108	82	26

ventured out were courting danger. Battalion commander Guo Qi, who went into hiding in the Safety Zone, later wrote a book about his experiences there, which contains the following passage: "The enemy soldiers were too cowardly to come out at night. Except for sentries who guarded their barracks, they were nowhere to be seen. We thus had ample opportunity to proceed with our own activities."[39] Judging from this account, it is extremely likely that crimes committed at night were the work of Chinese troops.

Chapter 6

Japanese Quickly Restore Order in the Safety Zone

A. No Women or Children Killed by the Japanese

All of Nanking's civilian residents, including women and children, had taken refuge in the Safety Zone, which was administered by the International Committee.

The Japanese occupied Nanking on December 13. The 7th Infantry Regiment from Kanazawa, commanded by Col. Isa Kazuo, was entrusted with the sweep of the Safety Zone. On December 14, Col. Isa stationed sentries at 10 locations near the entrances and exits of the Safety Zone, ordering them to prevent anyone from entering or leaving the Zone without good reason. At the Tokyo Trials, Col. Wakizaka Jiro, commander of the 36th Infantry Regiment, testified that when he attempted to enter the Safety Zone, a sentry refused to allow him to pass.[40] The fact that even a high-ranking officer was denied entry is evidence of how meticulously orders were followed.

As a result of strict orders issued by Commander-in-Chief Matsui, not one shell was fired into the Safety Zone, nor were aerial bombs dropped on it. No acts of arson were committed — in fact, there were no fires in the Zone. The Safety Zone was, as its name implies, safe. Rapes, assaults, thefts, and other crimes committed by a few renegade Japanese soldiers are described in records kept by the International Committee.[41] But no women or children were murdered, nor were any such crimes even documented. Furthermore, burial records prepared by the Red Swastika Society list virtually no women or children. It is possible that a few civilians were drafted to serve as laborers, or mistakenly apprehended during the hunt for Chinese military personnel masquerading as civilians. However, contemporaneous records describe the Safety Zone as, for the most part, a peaceful and quiet place. Consequently, every resident of Nanking was safe since, with a few exceptions, all civilians had congregated there.[42]

John H.D. Rabe, chairman of the International Committee, sent a letter to the Japanese military authorities on behalf of the entire Committee, which reads in part:

> We come to thank you for the fine way your artillery spared the Safety Zone and to establish contact with you for future plans for care of Chinese civilians in the Zone.[43]

The following are excerpts from a diary and notes kept by Dr. James McCallum, a physician associated with the Jinling University Hospital, which were read at the Tokyo Trials by Ito Kiyoshi (Gen. Matsui Iwane's attorney) during the presentation of Matsui's defense. They describe acts of kindness performed by Japanese soldiers.

> We have had some very pleasant Japanese who have treated us with courtesy and respect (December 29, 1937).

> Occasionally have I seen a Japanese helping some Chinese, or picking up a Chinese baby to play with it (December 29, 1937).

> Today I saw crowds of people flocking across Chung Shan [Zhongshan] Road out of the Zone. They came back later carrying rice which was being distributed by the Japanese from the Executive Yuan Examination Yuan (December 31, 1937).

Succeeded in getting half of the hospital staff registered today. I must report a good deed done by some Japanese. Recently several very nice Japanese have visited the hospital. We told them of our lack of food supplies for the patients. Today they brought in 100 shing [*jin* (equivalent to six kilograms)] of beans along with some beef. We have had no meat at the hospital for a month and these gifts were mighty welcome. They asked what else we would like to have (December 31, 1937).[44]

In *War Damage in the Nanking Area*, Lewis Smythe wrote:

The fact that practically no burning occurred within the zone was a further advantage.[45]

The late Maeda Yuji, former correspondent for Domei Tsushin[46] and former director of the Japan Press Center, described his experiences in Nanking in *Sekai to Nippon*.

Those who claim that a massacre took place in Nanking, leaving aside their accusations that 200,000-300,000 persons were murdered for the moment, assert that most of the victims were women and children. However, these supposed victims were, without exception, in the Safety Zone and protected by the Japanese Security Headquarters. The Nanking Bureau of my former employer, Domei Tsushin, was situated inside the Safety Zone. Four days after the occupation, all of us moved to the Bureau, which served both as our lodgings and workplace. Shops had already reopened, and life had returned to normal. We were privy to anything and everything that happened in the Safety Zone. No massacre claiming tens of thousands, or thousands, or even hundreds of victims could have taken place there without our knowing about it, so I can state with certitude that none occurred.

Prisoner of war were executed, some perhaps cruelly, but those executions were acts of war and must be judged from that perspective. There were no mass murders of noncombatants. I cannot remain silent when an event that never occurred is perceived as fact and described as such in our textbooks. Why was historical fact so horribly distorted? I believe that the answer to this question can be found in the postwar historical view, for which the Tokyo Trials are responsible.[47]

Accounts of the Nanking Incident in Japanese textbooks contain wording similar to the following: "Japanese military personnel killed 70,000-90,000 persons, if one counts only civilians, including women and children" (Tokyo Shoseki) and "Japanese soldiers murdered vast numbers of civilians, including women and children" (Kyoiku Shuppan). Every history textbook mentions that women and children were murdered in Nanking, but what is the basis for these claims? Even citizens of other nations that were antagonistic to Japan expressed gratitude to Japanese soldiers for maintaining order in the Safety Zone and for acts of kindness. This writer is unable to understand why Japanese textbooks contain accounts that distort the facts, and encourage our children to despise their motherland and their forebears.

B. A Letter of Gratitude From Another Refugee Zone

At this time, we would like to mention another refugee zone. About 1.8 kilometers north of Xiaguan, where bloody battles that claimed thousands of lives were fought, is the town of Baotaqiao. Over 6,000 refugees had congregated on the grounds of Baoguosi, a temple located in that town. The 11th Squadron, led by the flagship *Ataka* (commanded by Maj.-Gen. Kondo Eijiro), was sailing down the Yangtze on December 13. The fleet encountered heavy fire from a Chinese position at Liuzizhang, but finally broke through the blockade and headed toward Xiaguan. *Hozu* and *Seta* made up the advance guard, followed by *Kawakaze, Suzukaze*, *Hira*, *Ataka* and other warships. The Yangtze and its banks were crowded with boats and rafts carrying fleeing enemy soldiers, which the Japanese warships attacked. On December 14, the gunboat *Hira* anchored at Zhongxing wharf, one nautical mile downstream from Xiaguan. Her commander, Lt.-Col. Doi Shinji, decided to reconnoiter Baotaqiao. A munitions depot was located there, as well as a railroad siding, weapons, provisions, uniforms and other military supplies. Trenches had been dug all around the town, from which stragglers would often emerge, terrorizing the residents. Baotaqiao had become an extremely dangerous, lawless place. Lt.-Col. Doi voluntarily took on the responsibility of restoring peace and stability to Baotaqiao and its outskirts, whose 20,000 residents and several thousand refugees were living in fear.

First, Doi repaired the bridge to Xiaguan. Then he set about distributing food, clothing, and other necessities to the beleaguered residents. He changed the name of the town to "Pinghejie" (Town of Peace) and, with his men, protected the townspeople from marauding Chinese stragglers. Thanks to his efforts, order was quickly restored, but the most urgent problem, the lack of food, remained unsolved.

At the end of the year, the lead ship in a minesweeping operation struck a mine at the Wulongshan Fort blockade and sank. Doi, ordered to participate in the rescue effort, boarded the *Hira* and sped to the disaster site. When the rescue work had been completed, the *Hira* sailed to Shanghai, carrying a large number of dead and wounded sailors.

Lt.-Col. Doi visited Fleet Headquarters on the *Izumo*, then at anchor in Shanghai, and described the desperate situation in Pinghejie. Headquarters staff, moved by Doi's earnestness and sincerity, granted his petition for relief provisions. Food for the refugees was loaded onto the *Hira* and transported to the Zhongxing wharf. The ship arrived on New Year's Day in 1938. Chen Hansen, chairman of the local branch of the Red Swastika Society, a charitable organization, accepted the provisions, described below, on behalf of the refugees.

10 crates of preserved beef and pork
10 large bags of refined sugar
10 crates of dried fish
10 crates of soybean oil
10 packages of table salt
20 crates of dried rice cakes

To welcome the *Hira*, the refugees set off firecrackers. Each house sported a Japanese flag, and a banner reading "Pinghejie, Xiaguan, Nanking" was displayed at the town's entrance. The refugees and townspeople cheered when the ship arrived. A joyful mood prevailed.

On the following day, the town's officials put on their best clothes and lined up at Baguo Temple to receive Lt.-Col. Doi and his crew. Chen Hansen presented them with a receipt and a letter of gratitude (see illustration in P.41).

C. Funeral Services for Fallen Enemy Soldiers

On the night of December 13, the Wakizaka Unit (36th Infantry Regiment), the first to enter Nanking, cremated the remains of Japanese soldiers killed in action. Its members then erected a tall wooden tablet with a prayer inscribed on it in honor of the enemy dead, at which they offered flowers and incense. They buried the Chinese soldiers with respect, and chanted sutras for the repose of their souls all through the night.

The point we wish to make here is that there was nothing remarkable about the good deeds performed by Lt.-Col. Doi or Col. Wakizaka. They were simply demonstrating compassion, which was an integral aspect of *bushido*, the traditional code of conduct of the Japanese warrior. In fact, Staff Officer Yoshikawa Takeshi was severely reprimanded by Gen. Matsui, who claimed that the Chinese war dead were not handled with sufficient care. Could soldiers and commanders of this caliber have participated in or even condoned the indiscriminate killing of innocent women and children?

The Chinese have claimed that several tens of thousands of persons were massacred at Meitan Harbor and on the property of the Heji Company. However, Commander Doi steadfastly denies such claims, having never heard even rumors of such slaughter. From his testimony alone, readers should realize that this claim was preposterous propaganda.

January 02, 1938

To the Captain of the *Hira*:

I hereby confirm receipt of the following:

Preserved beef and pork:	10 crates
Refined sugar:	10 large bags
Dried fish:	10 crates
Soybean oil:	10 crates
Table salt:	10 packages
Dried rice cakes:	20 crates

The provisions delivered by the Captain are sorely needed by the refugees, and are much appreciated.

Words cannot express my gratitude to the Captain for his kindness and generosity.

Chen Hansen
Chairman, Hepingjie World Red Swastika Society Refugee Center
Baotaqiao Branch, Xiaguan District
WORLD RED SWASTIKA SOCIETY

計開

貯豬獸肉拾箱　糖拾包　塩魚拾箱

大豆白絞油拾箱　食塩拾包　餅乾弐拾箱

承蒙　艦長携帯食物多種賞賜難民足徵

艦長閣下恩典隆渥異常無任感謝

比良艦長　賞賜　世界紅卍字會下關分會寶塔橋收容所

平和街世界紅卍字會難民收容所主任陳漢森

昭和十三年新正月二日

Chapter 7

Report of Mass Murders of Prisoners of War Fabricated

A. Many Prisoners Released on the Spot

The most disputed aspect of the Japanese invasion of Nanking is the killing of prisoners of war. When, during a heated battle, a soldier sees his comrades fall, one by one, and realizes that defeat is imminent, he may decide that he does not wish to share their fate. He may throw down his weapon, raise his arms in surrender, and demand to be treated as a prisoner of war. However, there is no guarantee that his enemy will oblige.

We know from having examined officers' war journals that some of them issued orders to kill insubordinate prisoners, but that is to be expected in a conflict, as is the shooting of fleeing stragglers. According to the Rules Respecting Laws and Customs of War on Land, commanding officers have the authority to decide whether or not to take prisoners of war during hostilities. Commanders must make expeditious decisions, based on their instincts and training, because the outcome of the battle, their lives and the lives of their men are at stake. They do not have time to contemplate the possibility that they may be violating international law.

A Study of Combat Methods Used Against Chinese Troops, published by the Infantry School in 1933, contains a section entitled "Disposition of Prisoners of War." Fujiwara Akira's interpretation of the material in this section is that Japanese military authorities instructed their subordinates to refrain from executing Russian or German prisoners of war, but did not discourage the execution of Chinese prisoners.[48] Fujiwara has misunderstood the text, which follows.

> In keeping with our policy toward prisoners of war of all nationalities, it is not absolutely necessary to remand or incarcerate Chinese prisoners of war while waiting to see how the war situation develops. With the exception of special cases, prisoners of war *may be released* where they were captured, or after having been moved to another location. [Italics supplied.][49]

Nothing here states (or even implies) that killing Chinese prisoners of war is acceptable. It is likely that "special cases" refers to Chinese soldiers disguised as civilians. Chinese military personnel, unlike their German or Russian counterparts, commonly masqueraded as civilians and engaged in guerrilla warfare, even after their units had surrendered. The execution of such soldiers is not a violation of international law.

Any debate concerning Chinese troops disguised as civilians requires a knowledge of the Regulations annexed to the Hague Convention Concerning the Laws and Customs of War on Land (1907). According to the Regulations, soldiers wearing civilian clothing do not meet the qualifications of belligerents, which are as follows.

> Article 1. The laws, rights, and duties of war apply not only to armies, but also to militia and volunteer corps fulfilling the following conditions:
> 1. To be commanded by a person responsible for his subordinates;
> 2. To have a fixed distinctive emblem recognizable at a distance;
> 3. To carry arms openly; and
> 4. To conduct their operations in accordance with the laws and customs of war.[50]

Therefore, individual soldiers (or a group of soldiers) masquerading as civilians cannot be viewed as belligerents. Dr. Shinobu Junpei, Japan's foremost authority on international law, writes:

> In the event that a party who fails to meet the qualifications of a belligerent engages in hostile conduct, international law dictates that that party be charged with a grave breach of international law, punishable by execution or a lengthy prison sentence.[51]

Legal scholar Tabata Shigejiro concurs.

> Those who fail to qualify as belligerents do not have the right to be treated as prisoners of war when captured by the enemy. They are guilty of grave breaches of international law, and must be punished accordingly.[52]

Those who have embraced the "massacre" argument castigate Japanese military personnel for executing Chinese soldiers masquerading as civilians and carrying concealed weapons without benefit of trial. Perhaps they are unaware of the many, many instances in which Japanese soldiers were caught off guard and killed by those "civilians." In any case, the gist of the aforementioned section of the Infantry School document is: With the exception of those special cases, prisoners of war may be released.

It is true that, at that time, neither commanding officers nor the rank-and-file were not conversant with international law. Therefore, when faced with large numbers of prisoners of war in Nanking, they were at a loss as to how to accommodate them and, in some cases, they made bad decisions.

Such tragedies occur in all wars. To cite an example from the Western world, the portion of World War II fought in the European theater ended on May 8, 1945 when the Germans surrendered. Soon thereafter, 175,000 German soldiers were taken prisoner in Yugoslavia. While crossing the Alps, more than 80,000 of them were slaughtered en masse by Yugoslavian troops. Only about half of them were placed in detention camps. According to *The Prisoners: The Lives and Survival of German Soldiers Behind Barbed Wire*, written by Paul Carell and Günter Böddecker,[53] many other, similar incidents took place.

Hora Tomio conjectures that Lt.-Gen. Nakajima Kesago, commander of the 16th Division, ordered the mass execution of prisoners of war because the latter wrote "our policy is, in principle, to take no prisoners" in his diary.[54] Others, too, have misunderstood this passage and argued that Chinese prisoners taken in Nanking were systematically slaughtered, but that was not at all the case.

Onishi Hajime, former staff officer of the Shanghai Expeditionary Force, provided the following explanation about policy relating to prisoners of war.

> By "take no prisoners" Lt.-Gen. Nakajima meant that prisoners of war were to be disarmed and released. Chinese troops had been conscripted from all over China, but it was their country, and they could find their way home.[55]

Onishi added that no Division order (or any other type of order, for that matter) instructing that prisoners of war be killed was ever issued. Two detention camps were established in Nanking, housing a total of about 10,000 prisoners. Additionally, there was a small facility at Jiangdong Gate where model prisoners were detained, and two other detention camps. According to former Staff Officer Sakakibara Kazue, who was entrusted with the supervision of the prisoners, "I received orders to move half of the 4,000 prisoners held at the Central Prison Camp to the camp in Shanghai. I made the decisions about who would be moved." At the IMTFE, Sakakibara testified that "some of the prisoners were assigned to each unit as laborers. Many escaped, but we didn't try to stop them."[56]

When a new government (later headed by Wang Jingwei) was established in Nanking, more prisoners were released and reconscripted. Liang Hongzhi, who was instrumental in forming that government, and who served as head of its Executive Yuan, was eventually tried and executed for having collaborated with the Japanese. At his trial, he made the following statement.

> The Pacification Forces [appellation given to the new government's armed forces] were established in the spring of 1939. The majority of our soldiers were conscripted from the ranks of the prisoners. There were only a few enlistees. We formed four divisions, each consisting of only two or three thousand men.[57]

In other words, the vast majority of men who comprised the approximately 10,000-man Pacification Forces were former prisoners of war who had surrendered in Nanking or Wuhan. Liu Qixiong, who later served as head of the Beijing New Democracy Society's Supervisory Department, was once a prisoner of war in Nanking.

We shall now describe two cases in which prisoners were released where they were captured. The first involved the 20th Infantry Regiment (from Fukuchiyama), attached to the 16th Division and commanded by Maj.-Gen. Ono Nobuaki. Kinugawa Takeichi, a former member of the 1st Company of that Regiment sent a letter to this writer describing the particulars. An excerpt follows.

> We handled about 2,000 prisoners. Those who promised not to oppose or resist the Japanese were sent on their way after having been given a small amount of food and white flags. By the end of the year [1937], we had released about half of them. We put the other half to work: We had them wear armbands, and assigned them to transport food supplies and to prepare meals. Burlap sacks of brown rice found in a trench inside Zhongshan Gate were a godsend to our unit, but we were short of water and fuel. The prisoners were a great help in that respect. They worked all day long preparing food. I was in charge of them. They called me "Mr. Yi Chuan" [the Chinese pronunciation of Kinugawa], and as time passed, I became very fond of them. I never could have killed

> them. When we moved on to another area, we set all of them free.

The second instance involved the 45th Infantry Regiment (from Kagoshima), commanded by Takeshita Yoshiyasu. Approximately 5,000 Chinese soldiers waving white flags surrendered to the Regiment's 2nd Company at Xiaguan on the morning of December 14. From them the 2nd Company confiscated 30 cannons, as well as heavy machine guns, rifles, an enormous amount of ammunition, and 10 horses. Honda Katsuichi describes the release of these prisoners as follows.

> A great number of Nationalist soldiers, including Private 2nd Class Liu, reversed the position of their caps (with the visors at the back) and surrendered. There were several thousand of them.
>
> Once they had been assembled in one location, a Japanese soldier who appeared to be in command rode up on a horse. He had a full beard, three or four centimeters long. He gave instructions in Japanese, which Liu didn't understand. Through an interpreter, he learned that the officer had said, "You people are farmers. I'm going to release you. Make sure you go straight home."
>
> The Chinese soldiers were instructed to fashion flags out of whatever white material they could find. Private Liu took his handkerchief and tied it to a branch. The riverbank was strewn with clothing and household goods discarded by local residents. Liu replaced his uniform with some of the cast-off clothing.
>
> Once the several thousand Chinese prisoners had been freed, they set out for their home villages, carrying their white flags.[58]

B. Fourteen Thousand Prisoners Taken at Mufushan

The 65th Infantry Regiment (from Aizu Wakamatsu) under the command of Col. Morozumi Gyosaku, and attached to the 13th

Division (commanded by Maj.-Gen. Yamada Senji), took the largest number of prisoners (14,700), on December 14 near Mufushan.

To learn the truth about how these prisoners were treated, writer Suzuki Akira travelled to Sendai in 1962 to interview former Maj.-Gen. Yamada and other men who were at Mufushan. His report on those interviews, which we shall summarize here, appears in *The Illusion of a Great Nanking Massacre*. Maj.-Gen. Yamada thought long and hard, trying to arrive at an equitable decision regarding the treatment of the prisoners. Finally, he decided to transport them to an island in the Yangtze River and release them. However, when they had neared their destination, a riot broke out during which about 1,000 prisoners were shot to death. There were Japanese casualties as well.[59] The *Fukushima Min'yu Shinbun* carried a series of articles about the incident, which included the testimonies of many Japanese soldiers who were involved in the incident, under the title "Army Campaigns During the Second Sino-Japanese War." The series was later reprinted in a Self-Defense Forces publication.[60]

In its August 7, 1984 edition, the *Mainichi Shinbun* printed an article with a banner headline reading: "Former Army Corporal Describes the Massacre of More Than 10,000 Prisoners Taken in Nanking." The article relates the story of a Mr. K., a former corporal in the 65th Regiment, who marched 13,500 prisoners to the banks of the Yangtze and killed all of them. This was a major news story, since it stated that the executions were planned and systematic, contradicting the previously held perception.

Soon after the newspaper article appeared, Honda Katsuichi visited Mr. K., interviewed him, and wrote a two-part article, which ran in two successive issues of the monthly *Asahi Journal*.[61] Honda's articles, which contained more detail, asserted that the executions of 13,500 prisoners had been ordered by Shanghai Expeditionary Force Headquarters.

Mr. K. is, in actuality, Kurihara Riichi, a resident of Tokyo. He sent a protest to the *Mainichi Shinbun*, in which he stated that he had agreed to an interview because he wished to refute the charge made in *Testimonies: The Great Nanking Massacre* (supposedly official records) published in China, i.e., that Japanese troops had massacred 300,000-400,000 Chinese. However, the newspaper's reporter had both quoted Mr. Kurihara out of context and attributed statements to him that he had never made. Even though the *Mainichi Shinbun* didn't print his name, Mr. Kurihara felt that he had been slandered and exploited.

On September 27, in a tiny article bearing the headline "The Eyes of a Reporter," the *Mainichi Shinbun* summarized Mr. Kurihara's protest. However, the gist of the article was that the criticism that had been heaped on "Mr. K." was shameful. The newspaper offered no apology whatsoever for its reporter's misdeeds.

When I telephoned Mr. Kurihara, hoping to learn what he had really said, he responded: "Both the *Mainichi Shinbun* and Honda omitted the very points I wished to make. They twisted my words until they had me saying the exact opposite of what I had told them. I regret having spoken to either of them."

I telephoned him again, but when he wouldn't agree to an interview, I decided to fly to Fukushima and meet with Hirabayashi Sadaharu, former sublieutenant and commander of an artillery platoon attached to the 65th Regiment. Since Suzuki Akira's interview with Mr. Hirabayashi appears in the aforementioned *The Illusion of a Great Nanking Massacre*, we will print only the highlights of what the latter told us.

1. Many of my men were killed or wounded in the conflict at Shanghai. I was left with only one-third of the forces I had started out with — fewer than 1,500 men. To make matters worse, we were all exhausted. Confronted with prisoners of war who outnumbered us nearly 10 to one, we didn't know how we were going to manage to feed them. The first thing we did was to embark on a frantic search for utensils.
2. We constructed a bamboo fence around a school building at Shangyuan Gate, within which the prisoners were confined. The leaderless, weary prisoners were dressed in motley attire. Upon orders from Brigade Commander Yamada, we released

persons who appeared to be noncombatants — about half the prisoners.

3. A fire broke out on the evening of the second day. In the midst of the ensuing chaos, half the remaining prisoners escaped. Inwardly, I was relieved, but the fear of a counterattack was always in the back of my mind.
4. We used the black gaiters worn by the prisoners to bind them. They weren't very effective. By then, there were about 4,000 prisoners, but fewer than 1,000 men to guard them. Ours was an artillery unit, so my men didn't have rifles, only swords. We set out in the afternoon, forming a line more than four kilometers long. I was at the rear.
5. A riot broke out at dusk. Gunshots fired by escort troops were followed by a commotion at the head of the line that sounded like a combination of shrieking and screaming.
6. The disturbance soon spread to the rear of the line. As machine-gun fire reverberated, the prisoners scattered. With only swords to defend ourselves, we were very lucky to escape with our lives.
7. Calm had been restored by about 5:30 p.m., when we were visited by a mild squall. Then the clouds parted, revealing a bright moon, which illuminated the corpses on the ground — a ghastly scene that continues to haunt me.
8. At the Officers' Mess the next morning, I learned that an officer had been stabbed to death with his own sword, which a prisoner had wrested away from him. A dozen or more of my men were wounded, some seriously.
9. On the following day, all prisoners were ordered to bury the dead. As I recall, the work was finished in half a day. I heard that between 1,000 and 3,000[62] prisoners were killed. Many of the Chinese hid in the reeds, but we didn't attempt to apprehend them, and we certainly did not shoot them. If escape hadn't been the prisoners' main objective, many more of my men would have been killed.

The March 1985 issue of *Zenbo* contains the transcript of an interview with Mr. Kurihara, which is virtually identical to Mr. Hirabayashi's testimony. During the interview, Kurihara said, "When I read the article in the *Mainichi Shinbun*, I was astounded. They put words in my mouth. I told them my story because I wanted to protest the accusation that 300,000 Chinese were massacred, but they made it seem as though I support that claim." About Honda, he commented: "All he does is repeat lies the Chinese told him. I don't think he's in his right mind. I don't know why he bothered to interview me, because he made the whole thing up. I was betrayed."

Mr. Kurihara repeatedly expressed his anger at the *Mainichi Shinbun* reporter and Honda Katsuichi for misrepresenting him. For instance, he told them that he was in the process of transporting the prisoners to the opposite bank of the Yangtze, where they were to be released. However, in their version of his story, he was portrayed as the mastermind of a massacre.

The media are often referred to as the "fourth estate," because of the power they wield. When a major newspaper runs a sensational article and its editors realize they've made a mistake, they may print a retraction, but the damage has already been done. The fact that they slandered Mr. Kurihara by insinuating that he orchestrated the massacre of 13,000 prisoners was bad enough.[63] But far more reprehensible was their abuse of the freedom of speech, for the very reason that their influence on society is so profound. Irresponsible reporting of this sort distorts the perception of history, and insults and disgraces the Japanese people. One cannot help but wonder why these journalists are so intent on advocating a massacre that never occurred, disseminating lies that bring shame on Japan, and collaborating in Chinese propaganda campaigns.

Chapter 8

Chongshantang Burial Records Manufactured

A. Lies Exposed by Official Chinese Documents

In November 1945 the Chinese Nationalist government launched a citywide drive in Nanking to collect data that would support the IMTFE's case against Lt.-Gen. Tani Hisao (former commander of the 6th Division), and thus hasten his execution. To supervise the investigation, a committee was formed bearing the imposing name of "Committee for the Investigation of Japanese War Crimes Committed in Nanking: Procurator of the District Court, Nanking."

The members of the Committee represented both government and private organizations, including the Central Bureau of Military Affairs Committee, the Statistics Bureau, the Nanking Police Agency, the Lawyers' Association, the Physicians' Association, the Chamber of Commerce, the Red Swastika Society, and the Self-Government Committee, but not Chongshantang (a small charitable organization).

But the Committee's initial appeal to Nanking's population to come forward and attest to a massacre or other Japanese atrocities was fruitless. The city's residents "would give out no information."[64] The Committee accelerated its efforts to locate witnesses, conducting investigations "with utmost care, by means of various interviews and inquiries."[65] The result was the

"Summary Report on the Investigation of Japanese War Crimes Committed in Nanking," an excerpt from which follows.

> Just about the time of the fall of NANKING, our troops and citizens, numbering 2000-3000, were swept by enemy fire in the vicinity of YUHUATíAI before they could retreat. Sad wailing was heard everywhere; the ground was strewn with corpses and blood ran knee-deep. Meanwhile our troops and citizens attempting to escape by crossing the YANTZE [sic] River from the vicinity of PA-KUA-CHOU [Baguazhou] were swept by enemy fire. Many corpses floated on the water, dyed red with blood.[66]

This passage, however eloquent, does not constitute proof that more than 300,000 persons were massacred, and what it describes is a combat situation, not a massacre.

The report also contains accounts of sexual assaults.

> For amusement, a father was forced to assault his daughter. In another case, a boy was forced to assault his sister. An old man was forced to assault his son's wife. Breasts were torn off, and women were stabbed in the bosoms. Chins were smashed, and teeth knocked out. Such hideous scenes are unbearable to watch.[67]

It is possible that the Chinese derive pleasure from such assaults (they often lace their arguments with insults containing references to incestuous sex), but that is certainly not true of the Japanese, who have never found such acts amusing.

In any case, the Nationalist government submitted this hastily cobbled "survey report" to the IMTFE. The Court used this document as ammunition for its "Nanking Massacre" campaign, never subjecting the "evidence" or accompanying "testimonies" to even perfunctory scrutiny.

The year of Japan's defeat in World War II, 1945, marked the ninth anniversary of the Nanking Incident. The writer of an article that appeared in the December 15, 1945 edition of the

Shanghai newspaper *Dagongbao* expressed surprise that "offerings were seen at only a few homes, and that almost no one spoke fondly of the dead, expressed gratitude at having survived the war, or shed tears over the terrible tragedy that occurred nine years ago." The article continues: "When Chiang Kai-shek's organizations (the Nationalist Party and the Nationalist government) investigated enemy atrocities, they estimated the number of victims at 500,000. Why, then, are we seeing offerings at only a very few homes?" Why indeed? Perhaps because the "terrible tragedy" had never occurred?

The 500,000 figure was arrived at by inflating the original estimate of 300,000-400,000 victims submitted to the IMTFE, details of which follow.

Total number of persons killed:	340,000
Number of houses burned or otherwise destroyed:	More than 4,000
Number of women raped or killed after rejecting sexual advances:	20-30
Number of persons arrested and still missing:	184
Number of murder victims:	279,586
Location of Bodies	Number of Bodies; Witnesses
1. Xinhe District	2,873 (Burial workers Shen Shizheng and Chang Kaixing)
2. Near Army Arsenal outside South Gate; Huashenmiao	More than 7,000 (Burial workers Rui Fangyuan and Zhang Hongru)
3. Caoxiexia District	57,418 (Lu Su, a survivor)
4. Hanzhong Gate	More than 2,000 (Wu Zhangde and Chen Yongqing, survivors)
5. Linggu Temple	More than 3,000 (Gao Guanwu, a traitor; epitaph on the tombstone of an unknown person)
6. Total number of bodies buried by Chongshantang and Hongwanzihui (Red Swastika Society)	More than 155,300

If we add the figures shown in 1-6, they total 227,591, not 279,586, as stated above. The connection between 279,586 and the initial estimate (340,000) is unclear. The number of women who were supposedly raped or killed after they were raped (20-30) had multiplied a thousandfold to 20,000 by the time judgements were handed down at the Tokyo Trials.

The breakdown of burial figures is as follows:

Red Swastika Society	43,071
Chongshantang	112,261
Total	155,332

What is problematic here is the number of bodies allegedly buried (upwards of 155,000). Both the Red Swastika Society and Chongshantang prepared charts listing details of burials including city or town, date, sex, and sites where bodies were found. However, since these charts were created after World War II had ended, their veracity is suspect.

Nevertheless, the IMTFE accepted them without question. In its judgement, the Court describes the number of confirmed victims as follows.

> Estimates made at a later date indicate that the total number of civilians and prisoners of war murdered in Nanking and its vicinity during the first six weeks of the Japanese occupation was over 200,000. That these estimates are not exaggerated is borne out by the fact that burial societies and other organizations counted more than 155,000 bodies which they buried.[68]

Obviously, these burial statistics were used as irrefutable proof that there had been a massacre. Defense attorneys, of course, objected to the admission of this "evidence," on the following grounds:

1. The burial charts were prepared 10 years after the fact. It is not possible to make any definitive statements about corpses after

10 years have elapsed, so we must assume that these figures were invented.

2. In view of the sites where the bodies were discovered, they must have been those of soldiers killed in action. It is mistaken to assume that they were victims of a massacre perpetrated by Japanese military personnel.
3. These figures were, most likely, invented. For instance, Chongshantang supposedly buried an average of 130 bodies per day until the end of April. However, there is a sudden rise in the number of interments after April, to an average of 2,600 bodies per day for 10 successive days.
4. Yuhuatai, Shuixi Gate, and Zhongshan Gate were swept by Japanese troops, which would have removed or arranged for the removal of any corpses found. In any case, it is extremely unlikely that so many bodies remained at those locations five months after hostilities had ended.
5. Virtually no women or children are listed in Red Swastika Society records. But in Chongshantang records, figures for men, women, and children have been supplied so as to reflect the portion of the population each group accounts for. They were certainly fabricated.

Anyone who examined the burial records would have broached the objections raised by the defense. Nevertheless, the Court overruled those objections, and handed down a judgement defining all bodies interred as those of massacre victims.

This writer has harbored suspicions about Chongshantang for years. I asked people connected with the Nanking Incident, as well as those familiar with Nanking to provide information about the organization.

Former Col. Nakazawa Mitsuo (chief of staff, 16th Division) responded as follows, on the basis of his experiences in Nanking.

> The Japanese military undertook the main responsibility for burials, for which we hired many private organizations and a

> great number of coolies. The widespread perception that the Red Swastika Society and Chongshantang undertook the burial work independently of the Japanese military is incorrect. These charts were based on statements from coolies who took part in work supervised by the Japanese.

According to *Testimonies: The Great Nanking Massacre*, each Chongshantang burial crew consisted of 12 persons: a foreman, a regular worker, and 10 temporary laborers.[69] But as we mentioned previously, the organization maintained that it buried an average of 2,600 bodies per day. In an era when there were no bulldozers or power shovels, and when most trucks were owned by the military, how could Chongshantang have managed to inter so many bodies? Furthermore, no Japanese ever saw such a burial crew at work.

Recently, Ara Ken'ichi discovered some documents that further discredit claims made about burial work done by Chongshantang. All of them are Chinese records, and all of them refute assertions that Chongshantang buried 112,000 bodies between December 1937 and May 1938.[70]

1. "Statistical Report for 1935 Prepared by the Nanking City Government." This report contains a list of charitable organizations, on which both the Red Swastika Society (described as a branch of the World Red Swastika Society) and Chongshantang appear. Chongshantang dated back to 1797, but its main activities were supplying alms (mainly clothing) to the poor, and providing aid to widows and children. Nowhere in this report is there any mention of burial work.
2. "The Situation in Nanking: 1938."[71] Subsequent to the Japanese occupation, private charitable groups found themselves with almost no financial resources. In September 1938, the Nationalist government awarded subsidies to 26 organizations, including Chongshantang. But it is clear from this document as well that the organization had no connection with burials. Furthermore, Chongshantang is described as still active, but

on a very small scale. The following passage concerns burials.

> Disposition of Caskets and Dead Bodies
>
> Corpses inside and outside the city were disposed of by burial crews organized by the Red Swastika Society and the Self-Government Committee. Before the burial work commenced, caskets were interred by relatives. Unclaimed caskets and bodies were transported outside the city and interred.

Here again, there is no mention of Chongshantang. The burial work was performed only by the Red Swastika Society and the Self-Government Committee.

3. *Nanking*,[72] compiled by the Nanking Japanese Chamber of Commerce, contains "The Nanking City Government Service Committee: Statement of Income and Expenditures for May-December, 1938." This is part of a financial report for the City of Nanking, and states that the Executive Yuan expended 150,000 yuan in subsidies to charitable organizations. An accompanying chart shows that the largest subsidies (1,000 yuan per month) were awarded to the Red Swastika Society and Pushanhui, with seven other groups, including Chongshantang receiving 200 yuan each per month. The statement also reports that "private charitable organizations had been inactive for a time because the conflict in Nanking had depleted their finances. However, when they received subsidies from the Service Committee, they gradually resumed their activities." Chongshantang was unable to resume its activities full scale until September 1938, eight months after the occupation. This information is totally inconsistent with Chinese claims that the organization interred more than 110,000 bodies during the four months following the occupation.

B. Red Swastika Society Burial Records Unreliable

The burial records submitted by the Red Swastika Society in chart form are also suspect. In one section of the chart no burial site is listed, only "December 28: 6,466 bodies." This figure far surpasses any recorded before or after this date. Furthermore, according to the diaries of International Committee member George Fitch and Hamasaki Tomizo (45th Regiment), there was heavy snowfall on December 28.

The April 16, 1938 edition of the *Osaka Asahi Shimbun* carried an article that stated, in part: "According to recent reports, 1,793 bodies have been interred in Nanking, and 30,311 in its environs." When we combine these two figures, we arrive at a total of 32,104 bodies; and when we subtract the aforementioned 6,466 bodies that the Red Swastika Society claimed to have interred on December 28 from the total number of burials reported by the Society, we arrive at a total of 36,605. A discrepancy of 4,000 still remains, but Itakura Yoshiaki suspects that the figures for December 28, 1937 were manufactured by the Red Swastika Society. Hora Tomio disagrees. Last winter, a group of proponents of the "Nanking Massacre," including Hora, went on an inspection tour of Nanking. There they noticed that "on the original copy of the chart, which is housed at the Dan'anguan in Nanking, a piece of white paper has been pasted over the December 28th entry in the "Burial Site" column. Underneath the paper is printed 'Corpses dumped into Yangtze River near Xiaguan.'" Hora postulates that the Society wanted to conceal the fact that its crews had disposed of those corpses by dumping them into the river instead of adhering to standard burial practices, and that the 6,466 figure represents six days of work, not one. These are merely conjectures, however, and not evidence.[73]

An examination of a table in *Testimonies: The Great Nanking Massacre*, reputedly a collection of official Chinese sources, reveals that on December 28, 6,468 bodies were placed in caskets and buried at "Pude Temple outside Zhonghua Gate."[74] Citing this inconsistency, Itakura writes:

Xiaguan is situated to the north of Nanking, diametrically opposite the area outside Zhonghua Gate, which is south of the city. Further confusing the issue is the fact that, according to IMTFE references to evidence not admitted, including 15 photographs, those same 6,468 bodies were interred by Chongshantang.[75]

If Hora insists on attacking me because he is convinced that those corpses were dumped in the river, he must first prove that the aforementioned official documents are worthless. However, efforts in that direction will surely cast further doubts on the reliability of burial records.

We believe we have provided sufficient evidence to convince readers that the Chongshantang burial statistics are totally fictitious, and the Red Swastika Society's were inflated. In closing, we would like to add the following.

1. Most of the bodies buried were those of Chinese soldiers killed in action. The fact that only a few women and children are listed among the dead interred by the Red Swastika Society lends credence to this theory.
2. In the fall of 1937, thousands of wounded and sick soldiers were transported to Nanking from battlefields in Shanghai, Wuxi, and Changzhou. According to the diary kept by a foreign resident of Nanking, the city was filled with soldiers and reeked of medicine. Government buildings and even private homes were requisitioned to house them.[76] Soldiers who died from their wounds or illnesses, and those killed by aerial bombs should be accounted for as such in the mortality statistics.

Chapter 9

Professor Smythe's Report on War Damage in the Nanking Area

One of the most trustworthy primary sources relating to the Nanking Incident is Lewis S.C. Smythe's *War Damage in the Nanking Area, A Sociological Survey*. The scientific and rational methods used in its preparation raise it to a status unparalleled by any other contemporaneous reference.

Smythe, a professor of sociology at Jinling University, had conducted similar surveys in the past. During his tenure as both secretary and treasurer of the International Committee, he worked hard to maintain order in the Safety Zone and to establish good relations with Japanese military officials. On February 10, after transferring its duties to the Self-Government Committee, the International Committee disbanded. With the assistance of Professor Bates, Smythe hired a large number of Chinese students and, over a period of approximately two months, proceeded to conduct a survey on war damage sustained by the residents of Nanking. For the survey, Smythe used the random sampling method. He did everything he could to ensure that it would be meticulous, accurate, rational, and fair.

For the portion of the survey that focused on households, the students, working in teams of two, visited one out of every 50 occupied homes. They interviewed the residents and multiplied the figures obtained from those interviews by 50. For the portion relating to damage to houses, the teams inspected one house in 10. A certain amount of bias was inevitable, since the interviews were conducted by Chinese students, but the scientific methods used cannot be faulted.

Smythe's survey covered not only the Nanking city limits, but also Xiaguan and other areas located immediately outside the city's gates. The fieldwork was done between March 9 and April 2, and analyzed between April 9 and 23. The survey of buildings was conducted between March 15 and June 15. Smythe also conducted an agricultural survey in six counties adjacent to Nanking, from March 8-23, covering damage to crops, seed, farming equipment, as well as human casualties.

NUMBER AND CAUSE OF DEATHS AND INJURIES BY DATE

Date (1937-1938)	*Deaths by*			
	Military operations	*Soldiers' violence*	*Unknown*	*Military operations*
Before Dec. 12	600	—	—	50
Dec. 12, 13	50	250	—	—
Dec. 4-Jan. 1	—	2000	150	—
Jan. 14-Mar. 15	—	—	—	—
Date unknown	200	150	—	—
Total	850	2400	150	50
Per cent of cases of violence occurring after Dec. 13th		89		

* By "military operations" is meant bombing, shelling, or bullets fired in battle.
** Most of those "taken away" have not been heard from in any manner.

The survey results reveal that of the 3,250 persons who died as a result of the hostilities, 850 were killed during military operations. Soldiers' violence was responsible for the deaths of 2,400 and injuries to 3,050 others.

A table from Smythe's report, which we have reproduced as below, shows that 89% of the 2,400 deaths and 90% of the 3,050 injuries occurred subsequent to December 13, i.e., after the Japanese had occupied Nanking. The 4,200 persons listed as having been "taken away" may have been drafted by the Japanese to serve as stevedores or to do other types of labor but, as Smythe notes, most of them hadn't been heard from as late as June:

Injuries by		*Taken away***	*Total killed and injured*	*Per cent killed and injured by soldiers' violence*
Soldiers' violence	*Unknown*			
—	—	—	650	—
250	—	200	550	91
2200	200	3700	4550	92
—	—	250	—	—
600	50	50	1000	75
3050	250	4200	6750	81
90				

In addition to those reported killed and injured, 4200 were taken away under military arrest. Persons seized for temporary carrying or other military labor were seldom so reported. Very few of those here mentioned were heard from in any way up to June.[77]

Thus, those 4200 must contribute an important addition to the number killed by soldiers.[78]

Another table in Smythe's report (Table 5), which classifies the dead according to age and sex, lists the number of males as 2,400 (71%) and the number of females as 1,000 (29%). However, according to burial records kept by the Red Swastika Society, only 0.4% of the 1,793 bodies interred in Nanking were female. Therefore, though his survey was conducted in accordance with sound scientific methods, it seems to be marred by a significant amount of bias. Since bias of this sort would not result in an underestimation of the number of persons killed, the correct figures may very well be lower than those stated in his report.

Proponents of the "Nanking Massacre" have disparaged this worthy report, refusing to find any merit in it. Hora Tomio and others who share his views are convinced that approximately 200,000 persons (including 70,000-80,000 civilians) were killed in Nanking. They warn us not to "abuse" Smythe's casualty statistics.[79] Additionally, they object to Smythe's findings, i.e., that 2,400 persons were killed and 4,200 abducted by Japanese troops, for a total of 6,600 dead or assumed dead. Hora also cites the number of dead in the six counties surrounding Nanking as stated in Smythe's report: "Note the inordinate number of civilians who died."[80] But ironically, Hora has opted to espouse the theory Edgar Snow posits in *The Battle for Asia* — 300,000, believing this figure to be correct. Hora embraces theories that agree with his own, and discards those that do not.

Repeated requests on the part of defense attorneys at the IMTFE to summon Smythe as a witness were denied. The court would accept only his affidavit, which stated simply that he had indeed made the aforementioned survey.[81]

Witnesses were never punished for perjuring themselves at the IMTFE. Smythe wrote his affidavit in Nanking at a time when the Republic of China was engaged in a frantic, nationwide campaign to expose Japanese crimes. Smythe could have followed Bates' example and inflated or otherwise altered the results of his survey. The perfect excuse was at his disposal: His original figures were stated in order to placate the Japanese, who were in control of Nanking. But he did not. Smythe possessed the pride and conscience that one would expect of a scholar, as well as confidence in his work. *The Nanking District Court Prosecutor's Report on the Investigation of Crimes Committed by the Enemy*, which asserted that the "massacre" had claimed 340,000 victims, was prepared in February 1946. Smythe signed his affidavit on June 7, 1946. By doing so, he was indicating that his figures were correct; he never made any revisions to his report.

As we mentioned previously, the fieldwork for Smythe's investigation was done by teams of Chinese students who, equipped with safe-conduct passes, combed the six counties surrounding Nanking, and conducted in-depth interviews with farmers to determine war damage incurred. If anything resembling a massacre had occurred, it would have been reported to Smythe, Bates, or other International Committee members and, without question, included in Smythe's report. The fact that it was not is proof that there was no massacre.

Chapter 10

Gen. He Yingqin's Military Report

How do Chinese references describe the Nanking Incident? This writer is in possession of a copy of *Modern Chinese History: The Conflict With Japan*, published by Wenxing Shudian in Taipei. It was written by Gen. He Yingqin and edited by Wu Xiangxiang. The first printing was issued in December 1948, and the second in June 1962.

Neither the PRC government (not established until 1949) nor Chinese Communist forces had any connection whatsoever with the Battle of Nanking. Chinese soldiers who fought in that conflict were under the command of Chiang Kai-shek and his Nationalist government. Gen. He Yingqin, one of the top-ranking officers in the Nationalist Army, served as both minister of defense and chairman of the Military Affairs Committee. The aforementioned book contains the military reports written by Gen. He between 1937 (the year of the Marco Polo Bridge Incident) and 1945 (when Japan was defeated in World War II). The reports were submitted on an annual basis to the Legislative Yuan, a branch of the Nationalist government equivalent to Japan's Diet, for approval. They are detailed and lengthy, covering a total of 688 pages.

A statement in the book's introduction attests to the completeness and accuracy of their content: "The references included herein are exhaustive, and recount events as they actually occurred." The reports include several hundred pages of statistics and maps. The statistics list the number of soldiers killed and wounded in action in units of tens and hundreds. Military organization and combat conditions are also described in minute detail. Because these are also official records, they are primary sources, and probably the most informative and reliable Chinese sources available.

What did Gen. He write about the conflict in Nanking? This particular report was presented at an interim session of the Legislative Yuan in the spring of 1938, when the wounds of the fall of the Nationalist capital, Nanking, were still raw. It covers the period between July 1937 and February 1938. In its table of contents, we find: "Military operations conducted from the commencement of hostilities to the fall of Nanking." Readers are referred to Page 82 for an account of the fall of Nanking, which is very brief account (only six lines long) and, at first glance, seems almost perfunctory. However, organization charts and other specific information are provided in "Military operations conducted from the fall of Nanking to early March 1938."

The account of the fall of Nanking reads as follows.

> After abandoning the Xicheng line on November 26, the Supervisory Unit, the 36th and 88th divisions, and the 10th, 66th, 74th, and 83rd armies were ordered to assist in the defense of Nanking. Since all of these units had been engaged in combat for quite some time, their members were exhausted. They withdrew from the banks of the Suzhou River, and headed for Nanking. However, on their way there, they became involved in several conflicts, and were unable to regroup. The majority of 10th Army soldiers were raw recruits lacking combat skills, a factor that significantly reduced the effectiveness of that unit. Beginning on December 5, battles were fought at Tangshan and Chunhuazhen. On December 8, Tangshan fell to the enemy. Forced to abandon their position at Fukuo, our troops were pursued relentlessly by the enemy. All units engaged in intense, bloody battles. Many

men were killed or wounded. Unable to defend the last position at Yuhuatai on December 12, they were ordered to abandon Nanking. The enemy occupied Nanking on December 13.[82]

Note that there is no reference in this account to Japanese atrocities or a "Nanking Massacre." Also contained in the report are over 100 charts and tables containing detailed statistics for each battle fought, but these too are devoid of any mention of a massacre in Nanking.

According to this report, 33,000 Chinese soldiers were killed in action in Shanghai and Nanking (Combat Zone 3) and 65,340 wounded, for a total of 98,340. In those conflicts, 23,104 Japanese soldiers died in action and 50,000 from diseases contracted on the battlefront. In contrast, the Chinese figures seem low, but we have no reason to believe that they are inaccurate.

The Japanese suffered enormous losses in Shanghai, where most of their casualties occurred. Conversely, the Chinese lost far more men in Nanking than they did in Shanghai. In an entry in his diary, included in *The Secret Memoirs of Chiang Kai-Shek*, Chiang Kai-shek wrote that more than 6,000 Chinese soldiers were killed or wounded during their attempt to defend Nanking.[83] Chinese

Nationalist Soldiers Killed or Wounded in Action Between July 7 and

Conflicts in Shanghai and Nanking (Combat Zone 3)				
	Wounded	Killed	Total	
Officers	3,288	1,638	4,926	
Non-commissioned officers, rank and file	62,052	31,362	93,414	
Totals	65,340	33,000	98,340	

(Compiled by the Military Organization Bureau, Military Administration Department)
Source: *Modern Chinese History: The Conflict with Japan*, He Yingqin

propagandists habitually understated their own losses, while inflating those of their opponents. When Imperial General Headquarters announced the Japanese victory in Nanking, it reported 86,000 enemy casualties. This was an overstatement, but it pales in comparison to Chiang's understatement.

Again, there is not the slightest hint of a massacre in Nanking, much less one that claimed the lives of more than 10,000 Chinese, in this official, primary source prepared by Gen. He Yingqin.

This writer is grateful to Takagi Keizo, a China specialist who was intimate with Gen. He, for having supplied this reference. Takagi offered the following comment on the Nanking Incident.

> If tens or hundreds of thousands of Chinese soldiers and civilians were killed in Nanking, there would certainly have been mention of that in this report. But there is none. There have been many debates about the events that transpired in Nanking over the years. I cannot understand why no one has referred to this report, which is an official document issued by a nation with which Japan was at war.

Takagi's point is well taken. If the mission of the IMTFE had been to administer justice, these important references would have been admitted as evidence. Needless to say, the governments of both the Republic of China and the People's Republic of China are in possession of these documents.

However, Gen. He's report was not cited at the IMTFE. In fact, most of the evidence relating to the Nanking Incident presented did not derive from primary sources, or even secondary or

December 12, 1937

Nationwide Combat Zones 1, 2, 3, 5, 10		
Wounded	Killed	Total
9,810	4,884	14,694
233,142	119,856	352,998
242,952	124,740	367,692

even tertiary sources, but from hearsay, political propaganda, guesswork, and fiction. Figures supposedly representing the number of victims of the "massacre" ballooned until they took on a life of their own.

Even those known to this writer from books or articles published in Taiwan, Hong Kong, and Beijing vary wildly, as follows.

Sources published in the Republic of China (Taiwan) and Hong Kong

a. More than 100,000: *An Outline of the Eight-Year Conflict* by Chen Cheng, Army chief of staff, 1946
b. 340,000: *Nanking District Court Prosecutor's Report on the Investigation of Crimes Committed by the Enemy*, 1946
c. More than 100,000: *A Brief History of Chinese Resistance*, Ministry of Defense Department of Political History, 1952
d. More than 100,000: *History of the People's Revolution*, compiled from a variety of Republic of China sources in commemoration of the hundredth anniversary of the birth of Sun Yatsen, 1965
e. More than 100,000: *History of the War of Resistance Against Japan*, 1966
f. More than 100,000: *A Short History of the Sino-Japanese Conflict*, Defense Research Institute, 1968
g. 200,000: *Anti-Japanese Resistance*, Jiang Jingguo, 1978

Sources published in the People's Republic of China

a. 430,000: *Reform Daily*, 1945
b. 200,000: *People's Daily*, 1946
c. 300,000: *Worker's Daily*, 1946
d. 300,000: *History of China at War*, Shu Zongfu and Cao Juren.
e. 300,000: *People's China* (Japanese translation), 1947
f. 300,000: Government-approved textbooks currently in use
g. Several hundred thousand: *The Great Nanking Massacre*, Department of History, University of Nanking, 1948
h. 400,000: *Testimonies: The Great Nanking Massacre*, edited by the Historical Reference Research Committee, City of Nanking, 1984

1. All of these publications were written subsequent to the IMTFE, and are what I refer to as "sources created after the fact."
2. Inexplicably, most of the publications issued by organizations connected with the Nationalist government (the government in place at the time of the Nanking Incident) state the number of victims as "more than 100,000," while figures issued by PRC government-related publications range from "more than 300,000" to "400,000."
3. Figures listed in PRC publications vary, increasing every decade or so. They have been inflated for political purposes, and have no basis in fact.

Some Japanese actually believe these figures, and have begun to denounce the "Nanking Massacre." Their efforts in this direction are far more passionate and persistent than those of the Chinese. Furthermore, figures concocted to achieve political objectives now appear in Japanese textbooks. Will our descendants be forced to acquiesce to these figures for all time, even though they have been exponentially distorted? Surely I am not the only one who harbors this fear. Worst of all, these numbers are now being used as political and diplomatic weapons.

Chapter 11

No Mention of the "Nanking Massacre" in Chinese Communist Party Records

How did the CCP (Chinese Communist Party) and the Red Army perceive the Nanking Incident? The massacre of hundreds of thousands of Chinese would have served as excellent fodder for the anti-Japanese propaganda machine. And in their crusade to win rights for China's peasants, the Communists were battling another enemy, the Nationalists, and would have taken advantage of any opportunity to discredit them.

Beginning on May 26, 1938, Mao Zedong began his now famous nine-day lecture entitled "On Protracted War" at a forum in Yan'an held to discuss strategies for resisting Japanese inroads into China. Mao criticized Japanese military tactics, citing the hostilities in and around Nanking as an example: The Japanese succeeded in surrounding their opponents there, but failed to annihilate them. He did not, however, utter one word about a massacre's having taken place in that city. Nor do any other contemporaneous documents mention a "Nanking Massacre," though their authors do not hesitate to hold Nationalist negligence responsible for the fall of Nanking.

In connection with the absence of references to a massacre in Chinese documents, Takagi Keizo, the aforementioned China scholar, told this writer that such references are nowhere to be found either in Gen. He Yingqin's report or in PRC records.

> A book entitled *Chinese Military Affairs During Wartime* has been published on the Mainland. It is a collection of contemporaneous publications relating to Chinese military affairs, and includes Issue No. 109 of *Military Affairs Magazine*, dated June 20, 1938, which contains the earliest PRC account of the conflict at Nanking. The account reads as follows. "On the night of December 12, the enemy invaded Nanking. A fierce battle, waged on the city's streets, ensued. Ground troops were assisted by aircraft units. By noon on December 13, the fighting, much of it hand-to-hand combat, had become even more intense. Realizing that it was no longer politically crucial to continue to defend Nanking (all government organizations had been moved to Hankou), Nationalist troops decided to abandon the city in order to avoid incurring further, needless casualties." [84]

Readers will note that there are no allusions to the massacre of civilians or of prisoners of war by the Japanese military in this account.

The Japanese didn't know about the Nanking Incident, and it's quite obvious that the Chinese didn't, either — not the Communist Party, nor the Nationalist Party. Their ignorance is the strongest evidence that no massacre occurred.

Agnes Smedley, an American and the author of *Battle Hymn of China*,[85] was a Comintern member. (She was also the person responsible for having introduced Soviet spy Richard Sorge who supplied information to the U.S.S.R. that may very well have affected Japan's fate in World War II to Ozaki Hotsumi, also a Soviet agent, in Shanghai.) Smedley travelled with Communist Chinese leaders such as Mao Zedong, Zhu De, and Zhou Enlai. Her book is an account of her journey from Yan'an to Hankou. In it she describes the fall of Nanking and her impressions of the city, but does not refer to a massacre or to Japanese atrocities.

In the summer of 1938, a team of five Indian physicians travelled to Hankou on a relief mission. They met with both Nationalist and Communist party leaders, and kept records of their experiences. Besides describing combat conditions they encountered during their travels, the physicians also write that the

Chinese complained about Japanese crimes. However, they do not make any mention of a massacre.

In actuality, neither the Nationalist government in Taiwan nor the PRC government in Beijing voiced the word "massacre" until after Japan's defeat in World War II. Prior to the IMTFE, when the Allies unilaterally judged the vanquished, and to "trials" of Class B and C war criminals at various locations, there was no massacre. Not only the Japanese, but also the Chinese were hearing of it for the first time.

Himeda Tsuyoshi is the perpetrator of the Japanese translation of the aforementioned *Testimonies: The Great Nanking Massacre*, which purports to be a collection of official Chinese documents. In his commentary, he "explains" why there are no contemporaneous, official Nationalist or Communist records relating to a massacre in Nanking.

> Even after three of four years had elapsed, no references to the Nanking Massacre appeared in Chinese records describing the conflict with Japan. The most likely explanation is that the Communists had just united with the Nationalists to resist the Japanese, and the former refrained from mentioning the incident out of consideration for the latter.[86]

If the issue at hand weren't such a serious one, we might find this interpretation amusing.

In 1941, the Research Committee on Current Affairs in Yan'an issued a series of books entitled *China in Wartime*. One of the volumes, *Chinese Military Affairs in Wartime*, holds Nationalist troops responsible for the fall of Nanking:

> Who is to blame for the ruin and utter chaos in which our retreating troops were engulfed? ... How sad that a few high-ranking government officials failed to understand that moving the capital does not mean deserting it. They lost their ability to think clearly and rationally. In addition to alarming the Chinese people, their behavior made them the laughingstock of foreigners. [87]

Though the authors are unsparing in their criticism of Nationalist government officials, they make no mention of a massacre.

Returning to Himeda's commentary, another explanation he provides follows.

> Word of the Nanking Massacre did not reach ordinary Chinese citizens mainly because Japanese authorities controlled the media and prevented their representatives from writing or broadcasting news stories about it.[88]

If Himeda is implying that Japanese censors muzzled the Chinese government and the press, he is wrong. Even if they had attempted to do so, they lacked the power to silence the Chinese people. Not even a child would fall for this argument. In its Book Review section, the *Asahi Shinbun* described Himeda's commentary as "glittering." However, as the proverb tells us, all that glitters is not gold.

Why, after nearly half a century, is the Chinese Communist Party clamoring: "Four hundred thousand persons were massacred in Nanking.[89] ... Evidence abounds. We will accept no excuses?"[90]

Not until 1985, during the reign of Deng Xiaoping, was a memorial hall for the victims of the Nanking Massacre erected. The hall's facade bears the inscription "Victims: 300000." When the Communists came into power (1949), one of the first projects launched by Mao Zedong was the construction of a monument to Communist martyrs. The inscription on the monument reads:

> The Nationalist Government captured 300,000 Chinese Communist Party activists, brought them to Nanking, and slaughtered all of them at this execution site in Yuhuatai. This memorial park was created to comfort the souls of those heroes.

The political motives behind the sudden appearance of a monument to the victims of the "Nanking Massacre" with an inscription bearing the same figure (300,000), are patently obvious.

Chapter 12

No Protest Against the "Nanking Massacre" Submitted to the League of Nations

As we stated earlier, accounts of the "Nanking Massacre" in textbooks written for Japanese middle- and high-school students include statements such as "at the time, Japan was censured by the nations of the world." In this chapter, we shall proceed to disprove this claim.

Between 1920 and 1946, the League of Nations (the forerunner of the United Nations and the first permanent organization of its kind) attempted to resolve international problems. Neither the United States nor the Soviet Union ever joined the League; Japan withdrew subsequent to the Manchurian Incident (1931), and Germany and Italy not long thereafter. However, the United States maintained observer status throughout the League's existence, and participated in conferences held when disputes arose. Japan was asked to take part in several international conferences. By 1937, the U.S.S.R. was also an observer.

The matter of the Second Sino-Japanese War was brought before the Far East Advisory Committee during a meeting of the League's Assembly in August 1937. The United States was represented on the Committee; Japan was also invited to join it, but declined. As a result of a resolution adopted by the Committee, another conference was held in November of the same year in Brussels. Japan received an invitation from the Belgian government to take part in the proceedings, at which representatives of the

United States were present, but again declined.

At that time, League of Nations conferences provided a forum for participants to exercise their considerable debating skills in arguing international problems. When the Second Sino-Japanese War began, Chiang Kai-shek, with support from the U.S.S.R., used League conferences as diplomatic weapons against Japan. Not long before the invasion of Nanking, the Nationalist government had received a peace proposal from Japan. Instead of replying promptly, they dragged their feet, hoping that a resolution more favorable to them would be adopted at the League's Brussels Conference. They hedged their bets, so to speak, and by doing so, failed to issue a response in time to forestall the Japanese assault on Nanking.

Gu Weijun served as China's representative to the League of Nations. His League activities dated back to the Paris Peace Conference in 1919, at which the organization was established. From then on, he served as China's representative to the League. The Columbia University graduate had been endowed with a commanding presence, and his many connections in both the American political and international diplomatic arenas helped him garner success after success.

The League of Nations was asked to debate incidents involving the Japanese that had occurred in North China at the 18th Conference of its Assembly, which met between August 13 and October 6, 1937. These matters were submitted to the Far East Advisory Committee, which took China's side, and decided to hold a conference in Brussels, at which the Sino-Japanese Conflict Appeal was adopted. China also submitted the Resolution to Condemn Japanese Bombardment of Towns in China, in connection with Japanese aerial bombing of Nanking and Guangdong (Canton), which was adopted by the Committee and the Assembly. In fact, China issued protests to the League against every Japanese military action, which would invariably support the Chinese position, and pass resolutions condemning Japan.

The 100th Conference of the League of Nations' Council commenced on January 26, 1938, subsequent to the fall of Nanking.

During that conference, Great Britain, France, the U.S.S.R., and China formed the Sino-Japanese Conflict Committee. The Commission's members proceeded to discuss the possibility of international support for China. However, China failed to prevail this time, due in part to American apathy. However, on February 3, the League's Council unanimously passed a resolution promising support for China, with the exception of two nations, which abstained.

If atrocities were perpetrated by the Japanese in Nanking, as some would like us to believe, if Japanese military personnel indeed looted, raped, and murdered, and if the atrocities they committed were far more heinous than the bombing of Hiroshima and Nagasaki, then a protest would surely have been submitted to the League of Nations and, as usual, Japan would have been censured. But Gu Weijun never submitted any such protest.

The 101st Conference of the League of Nations' Council opened on May 9, 1938. China asked the League to censure Japanese aerial bombing and the use of poison gas during the conflict at Shandong. These proposals were adopted unanimously. But the League never censured Japan for a massacre in Nanking, accusations of which were never even brought before the League.

Judging from these events, it is obvious that the "Nanking Massacre" was a fiction created at the Tokyo Trials. In other words, there was no "Nanking Massacre" prior to the IMTFE.

Chapter 13

No Protest Against the "Nanking Massacre" from the United States, Great Britain, or France

What was the reaction to the invasion and subsequent occupation of Nanking in diplomatic circles? When Prime Minister Konoe Fumimaro announced that he would engage in no further dialogues with the Nationalist government, on January 16, 1938, both Japan and China recalled their ambassadors. However, the Chinese continued to file protests against Japan. In fact, after the Nationalist government relocated to Chunking (Chongqing) in November 1938, these protests became more frequent, taking the form of the Wang Chonghui[91] Declaration, the Chiang Kai-Shek Declaration, the Nationalist Government Declaration, and the National Assembly Declaration, to name some of them. However, the Nationalists issued no protest in connection with the Japanese occupation of Nanking.

During negotiations following two separate incidents in which the Japanese sank the American gunboat *Panay* and shelled the British gunboat *Ladybird*, Japan offered profuse, sincere apologies, and acceded to demands for reparations from the two affected nations. A variety of other protests were submitted by the United States, Great Britain, and France, all of which enjoyed considerable rights and interests in China. The Japanese responded to each and every one of these protests by issuing apologies and making reparations for damages. Housed in the Diplomatic Record

Office of Japan's Foreign Ministry is a long list of goods offered by way of compensation; it includes even automobiles and ships. The Ministry's gestures demonstrate how anxious the Japanese government was to avoid displeasing the Western powers.

Normally, when an international protest is lodged, it is signed by at least two nations. One and only one such protest, which accuses the Japanese of indiscriminate aerial bombing during the assault on Nanking, was submitted by the United States, Great Britain, and France on September 22, 1937. According to an investigation conducted by Lewis Smythe, about 600 Chinese civilians were killed by Japanese shelling and aerial bombing (see p.p. 62, 63). *New York Times* correspondent Tillman Durdin wrote that fires set by Chinese troops (the scorched-earth strategy) caused far more damage than Japanese aerial bombing, and that the Japanese did not fire one shot into the Safety Zone. The point we wish to make here is that not one of the many protests lodged even hints at a massacre or at Japanese atrocities.

The only explanation for this "oversight" is that no massacre ever occurred in Nanking. Nevertheless, Japanese textbooks state that as a result of the Nanking Incident, Japan was censured by the world's nations. We would like to ask the authors of those textbooks and the members of the Ministry of Education's Textbook Authorization Research Council exactly which nations censured Japan, and when and in what form they did so?

Chapter 14

No Mention of the "Nanking Massacre" in the American or Brithsh Press

A. Only Timperley and Durdin Wrote About Atrocities

As stated earlier, when the Japanese occupied Nanking, neither the Nationalist government (whose soldiers fought against Japan) nor the Chinese Communist Party accused the Japanese military of having perpetrated a massacre in that city. Not until the IMTFE began, 10 years later, was this accusation articulated. Nor did Western nations allege that a massacre had been committed. The vast majority of American and British journalists, in their coverage of Nanking, viewed incidents that occurred there as a breakdown of military discipline, not a massacre. Only two publications focused on Japanese misconduct.

One was *What War Means: Japanese Terror in China*, edited by Manchester Guardian correspondent Harold Timperley, and published in July 1938 by Victor Gollancz Ltd. A Chinese translation was issued simultaneously, under the title *Acts of Violence Committed by Japanese Military Personnel as Witnessed by Foreign Nationals*, and included a foreword written by statesman and scholar Guo Moruo. Both versions were intended to serve as anti-Japanese propaganda and were widely disseminated. *What War Means* enumerates Japanese "atrocities" in Nanking, and also contains reports written by foreigners on Japanese bombings in

North and central China. A portion of the documents prepared by the International Committee for the Nanking Safety Zone is included as supplementary material. After the end of World War II, this book was translated into Japanese.[92] The translation became the bible of Japanese proponents of the "Nanking Massacre." For instance, it is the first publication cited in Fujiwara Akira's *The Great Nanking Massacre*.[93]

Timperley was in Shanghai, not Nanking, at the time of the Japanese occupation. He had no firsthand knowledge of events that transpired there. His role was simply to compile documents that presented the Japanese in a bad light, which he had received from friends in Nanking. *What War Means*, like Edgar Snow's *Battle for Asia* (1940), which we shall discuss later, cannot be considered a primary source, based as it is on hearsay.

To support his view that *What War Means* is a reliable reference, Fujiwara quotes from *Shanghai Sojourn*, written by Matsumoto Shigeharu, who was head of the Domei Tsushin Shanghai Bureau at the time of the Nanking Incident.

> Matsumoto responded: "Mr. Timperley, as a Japanese, I am terribly ashamed of the acts of violence and murders committed in Nanking. Your book will turn its readers against Japan, at least temporarily, but that cannot be helped. We must offer a sincere apology to the Chinese people — to the entire human race, in fact. I hope that your book will remind us that we must do all possible to prevent a repetition of this tragedy. Thank you for your kind words."[94]

Fujiwara has quoted Matsumoto out of context. The passage he cites is preceded by:

> Timperley appeared at my office and announced that he had edited a book entitled *Japanese Terror in China*. He had the decency to add, "The book is anti-Japanese. There's no question about that. I'm sure that you will find it offensive, and it pains

me greatly to think that our friendship may be affected. The times being what they are, I didn't mention your name, but in my Preface, I did express my great respect for the two of you. Please accept this book for what it is: propaganda." [95]

More pertinently, the passage cited by Fujiwara is followed by:

> I purchased the book in June, intending to read it in its entirety. However, I was so sickened by the enumerations of incidents therein that I could not bear to read beyond the first half.[96]

Matsumoto had no personal knowledge of what took place in Nanking. Nor was his response to Timperley's announcement an opinion he had formed *after* reading *Japanese Terror in China*. The comments he made to Timperley were nothing more than the meaningless niceties that are exchanged at social gatherings.

Later, it became clear that Timperley's activities in China involved more than journalism. In *The Illusion of a Great Nanking Massacre: Updated Edition*,[97] Suzuki Akira writes that he found an entry for Timperley in *Notable Foreign Visitors to China: The Modern Era*,[98] which states that the latter was an advisor to the Nationalist Party's Central Propaganda Department.

Timperley compiled *What War Means* while he was under the employ of the Central Propaganda Department. Therefore, there is nothing strange about the fact that the Chinese translation was issued simultaneously, in July of 1938, to commemorate the first anniversary of the Second Sino-Japanese War. The book was intended to serve as propaganda for the Nationalist cause, and should not be perceived as the independent work of a Western journalist. We hope that proponents of the "Nanking Massacre" who have based their arguments on *What War Means* will come their senses.

Later, Matsumoto spoke to journalists Arai Kiyoshi, Maeda Yuji, and Fukazawa Mikizo, all of whom reported on the Japanese conquest of Nanking and its aftermath. The following is his report on their conversation.

> All three men agreed that it was difficult to distinguish between acts of war, acts of violence, and outright slaughter.[99] They also shared the conviction that no massacre of tens of thousands of persons ever occurred.[100]

The other publication is a two-part article written by F. Tillman Durdin, a correspondent for the *New York Times*, which appeared in the December 18, 1937 and January 9 editions of that newspaper. Though Tillman criticizes the Japanese military for its brutality, he is more critical of the Chinese, devoting more than two-thirds of his report to the Chinese "orgy of burning," the infiltration of the Safety Zone by Chinese soldiers dressed in civilian clothing, and acts of looting committed by the Chinese. But the statistics he offers for the number of war dead on both sides and the number of persons executed by the Japanese are conjectures, and do not coincide with known fact.

> In defending the city as they did — against all the dictates of modern military strategy — the Chinese allowed themselves to be trapped, surrounded and wiped out to the number of at least 33,000, about two-thirds of their army there. Of this number, it is estimated, about 20,000 were executed.[101]

Elsewhere in the same article, Durdin writes: "Japanese casualties during the actual siege probably totaled 1,000, Chinese casualties 3,000 to 5,000, perhaps more." Later, he adds:

> The Japanese themselves announced that during the first three days of cleaning up Nanking 15,000 Chinese soldiers were rounded up. At the time, it was contended that 25,000 more were still hiding out in the city.
>
> These figures give an accurate indication of the number of Chinese troops trapped within the Nanking walls. Probably the Japanese figure of 25,000 is exaggerated, but it is likely that

about 20,000 Chinese soldiers fell victim to Japanese executioners.

However, the main thrust of Durdin's invective is directed toward Chiang Kai-shek and Tang Shengzhi.

Certainly, General Chiang should not have permitted the blunder that occurred. Certainly, General Tang, too, is to be strongly censured for starting on a course of sacrifice that he failed to carry through or at best managed badly.

It may be that Tang made some efforts to save the situation on Sunday by arranging for a general withdrawal under protection of small units left to hold up Japanese penetration far into the city. Appearances indicate otherwise, and in any case the situation was not saved and Tang's departure, unknown even to many members of his own staff, left the army leaderless and was the signal for complete collapse.[102]

The Battle for Asia by Edgar Snow, who had already won acclaim for *Red Star Over China* (1938), was written three years after the Nanking Incident. Snow was not in Nanking when the incident occurred and, therefore, this book is not a trustworthy reference. It is intended to be an account of the Second Sino-Japanese War as a whole, and Snow's references to Nanking occupy only a few pages, which are essentially paraphrases of reports written by Timperley and Durdin. But Snow was a convincing writer, and *The Battle for Asia* was instrumental in propagating the myth of the "Nanking Massacre." (Even Hora has conceded that *The Battle for Asia* is a second-rate source, and that it contains errors.)

B. No Editorials Condemning the Nanking Incident

By the time Nanking was transformed into a battlefield on December 12, 1938, most foreign journalists had boarded the *Panay* to escape from Nanking. Remaining in the city were five journalists: Durdin (*New York Times*), McDaniel (Associated Press), Archibald Steele (*Chicago Daily News*), Smith (Reuters), and Arthur Mencken (Paramount News).

McDonald, a correspondent for the *London Times*, was temporarily housed near Xiaguan because the *Panay* had been sunk. He eventually returned to Shanghai (on December 17), but resurfaced in Nanking on December 15, where he reported on events there.

The claim has been made that the "Nanking atrocities" created a sensation overseas, and earned Japan the censure of other nations. Supposedly, only the Japanese knew nothing about it. In *The Great Nanking Massacre*, Fujiwara Akira writes, "News of the numerous atrocities committed by Japanese troops spread throughout the world like wildfire."[103]

If three or four of the world's tens of thousands of newspapers report on an incident, is that worldwide coverage? Did the nations of the world indeed condemn Japan? The Nanking Incident remained in the news only briefly, and was reported on by only a few newspapers. It is unlikely that the four wire services that held a monopoly over news from China at the time (Reuters, Associated Press, United Press, and Agence Havas) would have overlooked an incident in which hundreds of thousands of Chinese were massacred — an incident allegedly equivalent in magnitude to the genocide at Auschwitz.

Critic Ara Ken'ichi has embarked on a laborious enterprise, which involves searching the tables of contents of editions of the *New York Times* published between December 1, 1938 and January 31, 1938, *Time Magazine*, and the British newspaper *The London Times* for articles about the Nanking Incident. We regret that space constraints prevent us from printing the results of his investigation in full here. Instead, we shall provide a summary.

Most of the China-related reports in the *New York Times* in December 1937 dealt with the sinking of the American gunboat *Panay*. Accounts relating to this incident were on the paper's front page for two weeks (December 13-26). They appeared not only on the front page, but also on, for instance, pp. 16, 17, 18, 19, 21, and 24 of the December 14 edition. No other China-related news received this much coverage either before, during, or after the *Panay* incident. In comparison, only a few lines of the first installment of Durdin's two-part article about Nanking, its length notwithstanding, appeared on the front page of *The New York Times*. Nor were there any other front-page articles or editorials about the "Nanking Massacre" in that newspaper. Articles about the Nanking Incident were relegated to the Current Events section.

Between December 1, 1937 and January 31, 1938, the *New York Times* ran a total of 10 articles about the situation in Nanking, some of which were brief, one-column articles. Among them was one about Chinese officers who committed crimes for which the Japanese were blamed, an excerpt from which follows.

> American professors remaining at Ginling College in Nanking as foreign members of the Refugee Welfare Committee were seriously embarrassed to discover that they had been harboring a deserted Chinese Army colonel and six of his subordinate officers. The professors had, in fact, made the colonel second in authority at the refugee camp.[104]

From January 28-30, the newspaper printed articles describing the assault on U.S. Consul Allison by a Japanese Army corporal. But not a single article appeared describing mass slaughter in Nanking.

An article written by Archibald Steele (*Chicago Daily News*) describes the disorderly Chinese retreat and the panic that ensued when the Japanese invaded Nanking, and is essentially neutral. Durdin ends one of his articles with, "There was little glory for either side in the battle of Nanking."[105] He also mentions that the Japanese executed Chinese soldiers and committed rapes. Though the viewpoints of the articles written by the three foreign journalists remaining in Nanking are quite different, none of them even alludes to the massacre of civilians of any sex or age, or to mass executions of prisoners of war.

Ara Ken'ichi has made a list of *The London Times* headlines between December 12, 1937 and January 31, 1938. Since the British presence in China was longstanding, and British interests and settlements there were substantial, there was a higher level of interest in Chinese affairs in Great Britain than in the United States. Consequently, *The London Times* devoted more space to news from China, which made the newspaper's front page on the average of twice per week.

In December, the main news stories concerned the Shanghai Settlement, the assault on Nanking, the Soviet election, and the sinking of the *Panay*. Featured in January were the Spanish Civil War and the change of government in France. After exhaustive coverage of the *Panay* incident, Nanking reappeared in the news (January 15-16) in an article wired by McDonald from Shanghai. Some excerpts follow.

> Sunday evening [December 12] saw the first signs of the Chinese collapse, when a whole division began streaming towards the River Gate. They were fired on and stopped, and later it was learned that a general retreat had been ordered for 9 o'clock. The movement towards the gate leading to the Hsiakwan river-front, the only way of escape, was orderly at first, but it soon became clear that the Chinese defence of the southern gates had broken down, and that the Japanese were making their way northward through the city. The noise reached its climax in the early evening, by which time the southernmost part of the city was burning furiously. The retreat became a rout, the Chinese troops casting away their arms in panic when they found little or no transport to get them across the river. Many frantically re-entered the city and some burst into the safety zone.
>
> While retreating the Chinese fired the Ministry of Communications, the most ornate building in Nanking, built at a cost of £250,000, and as it was filled with munitions the explosions caused a tremendous racket.
>
> ...

On Monday morning the Japanese were still gradually moving northward, meeting with no resistance, and a systematic mopping-up had already begun.

...

On Tuesday the Japanese began a systematic searching out of anyone even remotely connected with the Chinese Army. They took suspects from the refugee camps and trapped many soldiers wandering in the streets. Soldiers who would willingly have surrendered were shot down as an example.

Young men who might have been soldiers and many police constables were assembled in groups for execution, as was proved by the bodies afterwards seen lying in piles. The streets were littered with bodies, including those of harmless old men, but it is a fact that the bodies of no women were seen.[106]

Photographs of the sinking *Panay*, taken by McDonald, occupied a great deal of space in the January 4 and 5 editions, but by the time he returned to Nanking, the situation there was back to normal. In any case, not one photograph of Nanking appeared in the newspaper, perhaps because there was nothing of interest to capture on film. And again, there were no references to a massacre or to mass murder. Other than those mentioned above, no other noteworthy articles about Nanking appeared in *The London Times*.

The *Sunday Express*, which reportedly sold far more copies than *The London Times*, carried two feature articles about Japan during that same period of time. The first (January 19) was a report on the sinking of the *Panay*. The second (January 23) was an editorial speculating about future Japanese foreign policy. The only other article printed described the assault on U.S. Consul Allison.

Returning to the American press, the weekly newsmagazine *Time* ran three articles that referred to the situation in Nanking. The first appeared in the December 27, 1938 issue. An excerpt follows.

At the last resting place of his old friend [Sun Yatsen] it was General Matsui's duty last week to complete the butchery of those Chinese troops, tragically misled, who, against the advice given by Generalissimo Chiang Kai-shek's German military advisers, had been left to defend Nanking. It was a tiresome job, lining up hundreds of prisoners and shooting them down batch after batch. However, according to foreign correspondents who witnessed some of the executions, Japanese soldiers invited Japanese sailors as their guests and apparently all of them "thoroughly enjoyed it."

All [the Chinese] knew that to be found in possession of a uniform or a gun meant death. Rifles were broken up and thrown into piles to be burned. The streets were strewn with discarded uniforms and munitions.[107]

This seems to be a reworking of the report Durdin wrote for the *New York Times*. Whatever the case, it does not describe a massacre.

The second article (February 14 issue) was essentially a reproduction of a report written by Archibald Steele for the *Chicago Daily News*, which read in part:

As the Japanese net tightened some of the soldiers went nearly crazy with fear. I saw one suddenly seize a bicycle and dash madly in the direction of the advancing Japanese vanguard, then only a few hundred yards distant. When a pedestrian warned him of his peril he turned swiftly about and dashed in the opposite direction. Suddenly he leaped from his bicycle and threw himself at a civilian and when I last saw him he was trying to rip the clothes from the man's back, at the same time shedding his own uniform.

The Japanese were bent on butchery. They were not to be content until they had slaughtered every soldier or official they could lay hands on. ... One Japanese soldier with a rifle stood over the growing pile of corpses with a rifle pouring bullets into any of the bodies which showed movement.

This may be war to the Japanese, but it looked like murder to me.[108]

The third article, a synopsis of material that had appeared in newspapers, appeared in the April 18 issue. The magazine's owners were obviously hostile toward the Japanese, since this article congratulated the Chinese on their victory at Taierzhuang, and included some pejorative comments about Japan. Apparently, *Time's* editors viewed the Second Sino-Japanese War as one of the top news stories, since they ran an article about it in every issue, in the "Foreign News" section. In 1938, they selected Chiang Kai-shek as "man of the year." But even *Time* never claimed that the Japanese had perpetrated a massacre in Nanking, nor did it accuse Japanese troops of murdering tens or hundreds of thousands of innocent women and children, or disarmed Chinese soldiers.

We have described the content of newspaper and magazine articles published in the two Western nations most hostile to Japan, the United States and Great Britain. Japanese "atrocities" never created a worldwide sensation. Japan was never censured by the nations of the world. Fujiwara's assertion is categorically false.

C. Foreign Journalists Inspect Former Battle Sites in Nanking

The American, British, and French media failed to write about the "Nanking Massacre" only because there was no massacre. Further evidence exists in the form of a tour of Nanking and environs by Western journalists, which took place in the summer of 1938, the year following the Japanese occupation. Members of the Shanghai Foreign Press Club had asked permission to visit former battle sites in Nanking. Japanese military authorities granted their request. A group of 15-16 journalists chartered a plane and flew to Nanking. The visitors set their own schedule, and inspected sites of their own choosing. Members of the Japanese military's Nanking Press Section served as their guides. The journalists visited the hospital and the detention center for prisoners of war in the former Safety Zone. Accompanying them was Domei Tstushin Nanking correspondent Koyama Takeo, who kindly provided his records of the experience, along with photographs.

According to Koyama, the visitors asked probing questions about the hostilities, the number of casualties suffered by both sides, the state of public order after the fighting had ceased, and prisoners of war. Then they discussed the questions and responses among themselves. However, they neither asked about nor discussed the mass slaughter of prisoners of war or the massacre of civilians. These men were not shy. If they had heard rumors about such incidents, they would surely have asked.

The group visited Zijinshan, Sun Yatsen's tomb, Zhonghua Gate, Yuhuatai, Xiaguan, and Jidong Gate, proceeding from there to Tangshuizhen and Mufushan. Not once did any one of its members ask about a massacre.

Koyama adds, "I arrived in Nanking in the spring of 1938, and was stationed there for more than three years. I never heard anything about a massacre. I covered every inch of the city while I was there, so even a rumor would have reached my ears."

Subsequent to the fall of Nanking, Gen. Matsui Iwane held two press conferences for foreign reporters. However, no one asked him about Japanese atrocities in Nanking. He also met with American and British military officials, on which occasion he apologized for the *Panay* and *Ladybird* incidents. During his conversation with them, no one broached the subject of a massacre. In an affidavit, Gen. Matsui swore that the first time he heard about the murder of Chinese civilians or the mass slaughter of prisoners in Nanking was on a radio program broadcast by the U.S. military in Tokyo. Dumbfounded, he summoned his subordinates and ordered them to conduct an investigation.

Chapter 15

No Gag Order Imposed in Connection with the Nanking Incident

The account of the Nanking Incident in one Japanese textbook states that "the Japanese people were not informed about the facts," implying that Japanese government or military officials issued a gag order prohibiting anyone from writing or speaking about the Nanking Incident. They did nothing of the kind.

The conviction that a gag order was imposed in connection with the Nanking Incident on the part of some proponents of the massacre argument probably stems from the fact that during the Second Sino-Japanese War (especially between late 1937 and the spring of 1938), the works of some writers were banned. Other writers were prohibited from publishing any of their work for a specific period of time. Still others were cited for violations of the Law Governing the Dissemination of False Rumors, but this had nothing to do with the Nanking Incident. Similar laws have been enacted by many nations in wartime, for obvious reasons.

Ishikawa Tatsuzo wrote a book entitled *Living Soldiers*, which was scheduled to appear in the monthly *Chuo Koron* in installments. *Living Soldiers* was banned as soon as the issue containing the first installment (March 1938) came out, on the grounds that the author had violated the aforementioned law. The text of the censors' decision on Ishikawa's case follows.

> *Living Soldiers* is a novel that tells the story of a unit of the Imperial Army, beginning with its experiences on the North China battlefront and ending when it lands at Baimaojiang in central China, in enemy territory, and participates in the invasion of Nanking. Almost every page is marked by hyperbole or portrayals that cast doubts upon the observance of stringent rules that govern the behavior of members of the Imperial Army, as described hereunder.
>
> 1. Scenes in which Japanese soldiers brutally and indiscriminately slaughter enemy soldiers and noncombatants;
> 2. Scenes that show Japanese soldiers looting in the South China battle zone, and create the impression that looting is an integral part of military policy;
> 3. Scenes in which Japanese soldiers assault Chinese noncombatants while robbing them;
> 4. Scenes in which Japanese soldiers violently assault Chinese women and girls in order to satisfy their sexual desires;
> 5. Scenes that portray Japanese soldiers as having lost the will to fight and longing to return home;
> 6. Scenes that depict Japanese soldiers as desperate men, both in thought and action.[109]

As readers will note, this ban concerned regulations prohibiting the slander of military personnel, and was not intended to conceal events that occurred in Nanking, regardless of their nature.

An examination of the regulations in force at the time reveals that a joint order from the Ministry of the Army and the Ministry of the Navy, issued on December 13, instructed newspapers to refrain from reporting on incidents involving damage inflicted upon foreign nations' ships by Japanese military personnel on the Yangtze River (the *Panay* and *Ladybird* incidents). The ban was lifted on December 15. Such orders were sometimes issued in advance, and at other times, when deemed necessary. However, none was issued in connection with the Nanking Incident, not by the Ministry of the Army, the Ministry of the Navy, or the Foreign Ministry.

Furthermore, penalties were imposed on three occasions in connection with newspaper articles about Nanking that violated regulations already in force governing the press. They concerned the December 17 edition of the *Osaka Asahi Shinbun*, the December 21 edition of the Tokyo *Nichinichi Shinbun*, and the December 25 edition of the *Kokumin Shinbun*. The reason: The newspapers in question had violated the Publishing Supervision Law, i.e., they had revealed military secrets by running a story about a canal's being constructed on the upper reaches of the Yangtze by Japanese naval personnel.[110]

In the process of collecting data for this book, we asked every former soldier we interviewed whether officers had imposed a gag order prohibiting them from writing about or even discussing the Nanking Incident. In each case, the answer was no. We posed the same question to former war correspondents, who replied unanimously that they were never subjected to any restrictions, save for restrictions they imposed upon themselves, something all responsible journalists do.

Chapter 16

A Massacre with No Witnesses

A. What 120 Journalists Saw

When the Japanese occupied Nanking, a city the size of New York's Manhattan Island, approximately 120 Japanese journalists and photographers accompanied them. Not one of them witnessed the massacre of women and children, or the mass slaughter of ordinary citizens or prisoners of war (with the exception of two journalists, Imai Seigo and Suzuki Jiro, whose accounts were fabricated). At that time, special correspondents for Japan's leading dailies (*Asahi Shinbun*, *Tonichi Shinbun*, *Yomiuri Shinbun*, and *Nippon Keizai Shinbun*),[111] local newspapers, and wire services were stationed in Nanking. To a man, these correspondents were shocked when accusations of a "great massacre" in Nanking were made during the Tokyo Trials, as were soldiers who had served in Nanking.

On August 31, 1982, Hara Shiro, Shanghai correspondent for the *Yomiuri Shinbun* at the time of the occupation (and then an advisor to that newspaper), made the following comment to a *Sekai Nippo* reporter.

> I didn't hear about anything remotely resembling a massacre in Nanking until three months after the city fell. Military authorities hadn't issued a gag order, so I thought it was odd that I should

> be hearing news like that long after the supposed fact. I contacted all our bureaus, but wasn't able to obtain any definitive information. Most of the people I consulted believed that the "massacre" was yet another Chinese propagandist ploy.[112]

In a book entitled *The Truth About the Conflict in Nanking: The Story of the 6th Division,*[113] published in 1966, *Tokyo Nichinichi Shinbun* correspondent Goto Kosaku wrote along similar lines.

> When the conflict in Nanking ended, I returned to Shanghai. Not long after that, I heard rumors that there had been a massacre in Nanking. Incredulous, I telephoned the Shanghai offices of *Asahi Shinbun*, *Yomiuri Shinbun*, *Domei Tsushin*, and other newspapers. Each time the answer was the same: "We haven't seen or heard anything about a massacre." I figured that this was another propaganda campaign launched by the enemy.

Recently, an article by Hatanaka Hideo describing his interviews of well-known military figures who had served in Nanking and entitled "Interviews Conducted in Nanking on December 12, 1937" appeared in the magazine *Sekai to Nippon*.[114] Of particular interest is the following exchange between Hatanaka and Ishikawa Tatsuzo, which took place shortly before the latter's death. As mentioned previously, Ishikawa's novel *Living Soldiers* was censored, and the author did actually receive a prison sentence, though he was granted probation.

Ishikawa: I went to Nanking two weeks after the ceremonial entry.
Hatanaka: What sort of atrocities did you witness?
Ishikawa: I saw no signs of a massacre — not one.
Hatanaka: What are your views on the "Nanking Massacre?"
Ishikawa: It would have been impossible to dispose of tens of thousands of bodies in two or three weeks. Even today, I'm convinced that no massacre ever took place.[115]

Ishikawa's words are of particular importance for the very reason that his book was censored, and he was treated like a criminal. In his book *The Road to Nanking*,[116] Honda Katsuichi cites *Living Soldiers*, referring to it as a source of powerful evidence that a massacre did indeed take place in Nanking, an action that must have infuriated Ishikawa.

Hatanaka also interviewed Hashimoto Tomisaburo, a colorful figure who headed the Shanghai Bureau of the *Asahi Shinbun* in the late 1930's. During the Tanaka administration, Hashimoto served as secretary-general of the LDP,[117] and as transport minister. Hashimoto and his team of 15 reporters were the first journalists to enter Nanking after the Japanese occupation. His response to a question posed by Hatanaka follows.

> The Nanking Incident? Never heard a thing about it. If anything like that had happened, reporters would have talked about it, you can bet on that. After all, news is their business. I never even heard rumors of a massacre. We held meetings attended by every *Asahi Shinbun* reporter based in the area. If there had been a massacre, someone would have mentioned it, and even if they didn't call it a massacre, our reporters would certainly have voiced objections.

Hatanaka also interviewed Adachi Kazuo, the former Nanking correspondent for the *Asahi Shinbun*. When Hatanaka telephoned him to ask about the "massacre," Adachi's reply was curt: "I saw no evidence of a massacre in Nanking. I have no idea who you are, but if you want me to attest to a massacre in Nanking, I cannot help you."

After a brief exchange during which Hatanaka identified himself and explained why he had contacted Adachi, the latter agreed to an interview. Hatanaka asked about former *Asahi Shinbun* reporter Imai Seigo, who claimed to have witnessed a massacre. Adachi's comment was: "Imai wasn't in the habit of reporting on what he had actually seen. His talent lay in dramatizing stories he had heard from others."

In a roundabout way, Adachi was suggesting that an article that appeared in *Bungei Shunju*, in which Imai claimed to have witnessed the massacre of 20,000 persons, was suspect. His appraisal is identical to that provided to this writer by Moriyama Takashi, also of the *Asahi Shimbun*. Moriyama should know, since he shared a room with Imai in Nanking, and the two reported as a team. Imai never mentioned anything about a massacre to him.

B. Testimonies of Japanese Soldiers and Journalists

An eight-part series entitled "Japanese Witnesses to the Fall of Nanking," written by Ara Ken'ichi, appeared in the magazine *Seiron*, beginning in May 1986. Ara conducted exhaustive interviews with newspaper reporters, photographers, and soldiers who witnessed the fall of Nanking. He then compiled them into article form, without alteration. Due to space limitations, rather than providing a detailed analysis of this series, we will limit our discussion to the "massacre." The numbers that follow refer to the installments cited.

1. Onishi Hajime, former captain and staff officer of the Shanghai Expeditionary Forces

Onishi, the first person Ara interviewed, was the youngest intelligence officer in the 2nd Section. For approximately one year, he served as head of the Nanking Special Agency.

Onishi: I served under Cho Isamu. If he issued an order [instructing his men to kill prisoners of war], I never saw it, nor did I hear anything about it ... in any case, it would have been extraordinary for someone in his position to give orders of that sort.

Ara: In his diary, Gen. Nakajima (Kesago), commander of the 16th Division, wrote: "Our policy is to take no prisoners." Some say that this passage is proof that prisoners of war were massacred.

Onishi: "Take no prisoners" meant that we were supposed to disarm them and let them go. The Chinese soldiers came from all over China, but it was their country, so they could walk home.

Ara: Did anyone in the Shanghai Expeditionary Forces mention that there had been a massacre?

Onishi: No, the subject was never broached. Once I entered Nanking, I made rounds of the city, ensuring that military discipline and regulations were observed.

Ara: And you saw nothing?

Onishi: I witnessed a rape once.

2. Okada Takashi, former Army interpreter for Commander-in-Chief Matsui

There weren't any corpses within the city, so I don't think any atrocities were committed against civilians.

They say that there were fires, but I don't remember any.

I did hear stories about prisoners of war. I heard that someone had tried to transport them from Xiaguan to the opposite bank of the Yangtze ... while they were crossing the river, chaos erupted and some of the prisoners were shot.

Okada Yuji, former major and Special Services officer, Shanghai Expeditionary Forces

During the conflict that ensued when we invaded Nanking, I noticed that some of the Chinese soldiers were women. I saw a dead female Chinese soldier. Some of the stragglers resisted, and then there were soldiers who weren't wearing uniforms. I saw some of them being executed. Perhaps people saw their corpses afterwards, and that's how the massacre rumor got started.

3. Sato Shinju, former *Tokyo Nichinichi Shinbun* photographer

Ara: They say there was a massacre.

Sato: I didn't see it. That's what they say, but by the 16th or 17th [of December 1937], street vendors were back in business. Not just in back alleys, but on main streets, too. Also, a lot of Chinese people were wearing armbands with the Japanese flag on them, and congregating around Japanese soldiers. I don't think they would have done that if Chinese people had been killed indiscriminately.

Ara: When did you first hear about the Nanking Incident?

Sato: Not until after World War II. It was during the American occupation, so it must have been 1946 or 1947. There was a radio program on NHK produced by the GHQ called "Box of Truth." On one of them I heard that there had been a massacre in Nanking. That was the first time I heard about it.

Asai Tatsuzo, former photographer for the Motion Picture Department of Domei Tsushin

Ara: Was there talk of a massacre or anything like that among the Domei Tsushin staff?

Asai: No, not a bit. There were a lot of stragglers, and soldiers in civilian clothing. We believed that getting rid of [executing] them was an unavoidable aspect of war.

4. Taguchi Toshisuke, *Hochi Shinbun* war correspondent

Ara: They say that a massacre was perpetrated in Nanking.

Taguchi: I never heard about it while I was there. No one

ever mentioned it.

Hosonami Takashi, former wireless engineer, Domei Tsushin

Hosonami: There were corpses in the pillboxes, and also on the banks of the Yangtze. Some of them had been bound together with wire.
Ara: How many bodies were there?
Hosonami: About 100, I guess. They must have killed prisoners of war who were in Tangshan.

5. Koike Shuyo, *Miyako Shinbun* reporter (entered Nanking on December 13)

Koike: All the houses in Nanking had been abandoned, so the city was deserted. You didn't hear a sound. There was a weird, ghostly air about the place — I didn't see one cat or dog. I was shocked because the streets were so still and silent. You would never have known that a battle had been fought there.
Ara: What was the situation in the Safety Zone?
Koike: The refugees were upset when Japanese soldiers searched for stragglers but, generally, the Safety Zone was peaceful. There wasn't any food. The refugees were starving, and would beg us for food. I found several sacks of rice at our lodgings, so I told one of the Safety Zone leaders to go there with me. I gave him enough rice and other food to fill two large carts. But there were 60 or 70 thousand people in the Refugee Zone, so I don't think my contribution made much of a difference.
Ara: They say that there was a massacre in Nanking. Did you see corpses that might have led you to believe that one had occurred?
Koike: I don't know if they were massacred, or died in

battle, but there were several bodies in the basement of a building that was under construction, near the central traffic circle ... also, on my way to Yijiang Gate, I believe, in a truck, I saw a body that had been squashed flat. It looked as though it had been repeatedly run over ... at the docks at Xiaguan, there was a shipyard, circular in shape, that looked like a stadium. I saw piles of bodies that had been dumped there.

Ara: About how many bodies did you see at the docks?

Koike: More than five or 10 — maybe several dozen. I think they were corpses of soldiers who had died in battle.

Ara: Were there other bodies there?

Koike: No.

Koike also mentioned that he had noticed a fire on Zhongzheng Road on December 13. This is crucial evidence, since on that same occasion, he saw foreign reporters traveling in two automobiles driving all around the city at full speed, the shutters of their cameras clicking away. This information contradicts the widespread perception that Japanese military authorities did not grant foreign journalists access to Nanking.

Higuchi Tetsuo, former *Yomiuri Shinbun* engineer

Higuchi: Since I had an automobile, I drove around the city every day.

Ara: They say that the Japanese military perpetrated a massacre at about that time.

Higuchi: Well, I don't know anything about that.

Ara: You didn't see it taking place or hear about it?

Higuchi: I had no idea. I saw absolutely no evidence of a massacre. Yes, they say that one occurred, but I don't know where or how. The Zhongshan Mausoleum and similar sites were intact. They hadn't been desecrated. I think that our soldiers killed people only when their lives were in danger, and they're calling that a massacre.

6. Kanazawa Yoshio, former photographer, *Tokyo Nichinichi Shinbun*

After World War II, I heard that tens of thousands of people were slaughtered in Nanking. I couldn't believe my ears. When I was in Nanking, I walked all around the city, but I never saw or heard any signs of a massacre.

I was there for about a month, but I neither saw nor heard anything that would support the accusations I heard after the war. There couldn't have been a massacre. I simply cannot understand why they executed General Matsui.

Mori Hiroshi, Shanghai correspondent, *Yomiuri Shinbun*

The residents of Nanking were not hostile to us, and they didn't seem to be afraid of Japanese soldiers. Quite the opposite — Japanese military personnel were wary of the Chinese because soldiers masqueraded as civilians.

Japanese soldiers did take prisoners, but there wasn't enough food to feed them, or facilities to house them. If they had let them go, the prisoners would have resumed military activity. They said they really didn't have any choice but to execute them. An NCO issued the orders — a squad leader, I think.

7. Tani Isamu, former colonel and chief of staff, 10th Army

Tani: When I entered the city through Zhonghua Gate at about 11:30 a.m. on December 14, I saw very few bodies there. At about 3:00 p.m. I thought that, as commander of the Rear Section, I should inspect the occupied area. Accompanied by a sentry squad from Headquarters, we made the rounds of the city in automobiles. When we arrived at Xiaguan, there was a warship moored there. I met with the captain. There were quite a few corpses on that bank, perhaps 1,000, perhaps even two or three thousand. More than half of them were clad in uniforms. The others were dressed as civilians.

Ara: Were they killed during the conflict?

Tani: I think they were shot by the 16th Division while attempting to escape from the city. Perhaps that was what was later referred to as a massacre.

Ara: I've been told that there were corpses at Yijiang Gate as well. Did you see them?

Tani: Someone wrote that there were a great many bodies at Yijiang Gate. I went by there on the afternoon of the 14th, but there were no corpses there at that time.

Tani opened his scrapbook, which contains a photograph of Yijiang Gate taken on December 14. The photograph shows the gate with its three entrances, but there is not a single corpse in sight.

Tani: I also heard that there was a massacre at Yuhuatai, but there were no bodies there, either.

Yoshinaga Sunao, former major and operations staff officer, 10th Army

Yoshinaga: I entered Nanking on the morning of December 13, through Zhonghua Gate.

Ara: What was the situation in Nanking then?

Yoshinaga: On my way to Chubei Bank, I encountered a Chinese family. They didn't arouse my suspicions, so I wrote a note on the back of my business card indicating that they should be permitted to cross the sentry line and handed it to them. Since families felt that it was safe enough to walk about the city that day (December 13), the situation in Nanking had obviously calmed down quite a bit.

Two or three days later I went to Xiaguan, on an operation. There were quite a few dead Chinese soldiers on the wharf at the Yangtze River — several thousand, perhaps. The 10th Army (the Kunisaki Detachment) had attacked not only from the south side of Nanking, but also from Pukou, so the corpses must have belonged to soldiers killed during those attacks.

8. Kaneko Rinsuke, former captain and staff officer, 10th Army

Kaneko: I entered Nanking on the 13th or 14th. I didn't see one corpse in the city, nor did I hear a single shot fired.

Ara: Then you heard nothing about a massacre at the time?

Kaneko: That's right. Not a thing. When I heard about it at the Tokyo Trials, I was astounded. I'm not trying to hide anything or hold anything back. The truth is that I saw nothing of the kind in Nanking, nothing that would leave an impression of that sort.

Futamura Jiro, former photographer, *Hochi Shinbun*

Ara: There's been talk of a massacre in Nanking.

Futamura: I didn't see anything like that when I was there. After World War II, I was often asked about it. I resurrected my memories of the time I spent there, but I had to ask the inquirers what they meant by

> "massacre." I have read what others have written about it. But there wasn't any site where people were murdered en masse like Auschwitz, you know. The first I heard about it was when the Tokyo Trials were held.

C. Writers' and critics' accounts of their experiences in Nanking

Approximately 120 journalists and photographers entered Nanking subsequent to the Japanese occupation. However, they were not the only Japanese civilians to visit the city. Renowned commentators, writers, and poets, including Oya Soichi,[118] Kimura Ki, Sugiyama Heisuke, Noyori Hideichi, Saijo Yaso,[119] Kusano Shinpei,[120] Hayashi Fumiko,[121] and Ishikawa Tatsuzo were in Nanking when that city fell, or soon thereafter. Many other distinguished members of society spent time there during the spring and summer of 1938. Upon their return to Japan, all these visitors wrote reports describing their experiences, which appeared in magazines and newspapers. Some of them gave lectures.

For instance, Sugiyama Heisuke wrote a series entitled "Nanking" for the *Asahi Shinbun*. Kimura Ki wrote *Early Spring in Jiangnan* and Hayashi Fumiko, *Journey to Nanking*. Kobayashi Hideo[122] penned *From Hangzhou to Nanking*. On the spur of the moment, poet Kusano Shinpei and Noyori Hideichi, president of the company that published *Business World*, travelled to Nanking together. Later, the former wrote *A Land of Peace and Turmoil*, which appeared in *Business World*, and the latter, *Travels in China*. Both men spent a good deal of time exploring Nanking and its environs, on foot and by car. Their accounts are vivid and detailed. However, none of the aforementioned accounts hints, even remotely, at a massacre.

Not long after World War II ended, the Tokyo Trials began. But even when criticism of the Japanese military and its tactics reached its peak, not one of these literary figures came forth with accusations of a "Nanking Massacre." The inimitable Oya Soichi, who was superbly capable of trenchant criticism, both oral and written, was no exception. As long as he lived, Oya dismissed accusations of a Nanking massacre.

D. What This Writer Saw in Nanking

This writer, too, visited Nanking in July 1938, subsequent to the Nanking Incident. I spent about a month in that city, on assignment for Pan-Asia magazine. In August, along with Hayashi Fumiko and a few others, I travelled with the 6th Division units headquartered on the right bank of the Yangtze, beginning with the invasion of Hankou in August. In October, our party was with the first unit to attack Wuhan.

Gen. Matsui Iwane, who was also chairman of the Pan-Asian Association, had instructed me to inspect the Nanking area, mainly to gauge the degree of public safety and the residents' reactions to the occupation. He had given me several letters of introduction. I was just a war correspondent, but the heads of the Nanking Special Agency and the Press Bureau went out of their way to assist me, ensuring that I saw every inch of the city. I visited Tangshuizhen, Xianhemenzhen, Jurong, and Pukou, as well as former battle sites in Nanking and areas in the city's immediate environs, including Xiaguan, Yuhuatai, and Zijinshan. My lodgings were in a communications barracks near the Drum Tower, which was located right at the entrance to the Safety Zone. Sentries were still posted there, checking civilian passports. Inside the Safety Zone, I saw the infamous thieves' markets, street hawkers, and row upon row of vendors' stalls. The Safety Zone was a beehive of activity, and Dafang Alley and similar places were bustling from early morning till night. By that time, the population had swelled to nearly 500,000. I even spotted female employees of Japanese-owned restaurants walking through the streets of Zouhui, Nanking's red-light district, clad in summer kimono.

According to testimony given at the Tokyo Trials and reports issued by the International Committee, acts of arson committed by Japanese soldiers had reduced more than one-third of the city to ashes. However, these claims were patently false. With the exception of Xiaguan, I saw much less evidence of destruction by fire than I had anticipated. In fact, I was surprised to find the city in such an orderly state.

Needless to say, I heard no rumors to the effect that a massacre had occurred in Nanking seven months prior to my arrival, though I was told, everywhere I visited, about the bloody battles that had ensued when the Japanese invaded the city. I will never forget the stories I was told about the brave Chinese soldiers who chained themselves to the pillboxes at Yuhuatai, and continued to fire their guns until they died, or the sight of the chains, which were shown to me.

The majority of war correspondents, photographers, writers, and poets who spent time in Nanking are united in their insistence that they neither saw nor heard any signs of a Nanking massacre until the Tokyo Trials commenced.

Further proof was supplied by Hosokawa Ryugen, former reporter and managing editor of the *Asahi Shinbun*, and then a political and social critic with an immense following. In 1986, on the Sunday preceding the anniversary of the end of World War II (August 14), Hosokawa appeared on "Candid Conversations About Current Events" aired by TBS (Tokyo Broadcasting System). Some of his comments follow.

> When I was managing editor of the *Asahi Shinbun*, I assembled all the reporters who had been assigned to Nanking and asked them, individually, whether they had heard any rumors about a massacre in Nanking. And every single one of them replied, in no uncertain terms, that he had neither seen or heard anything to that effect ... I can state with certainty that no massacre occurred in which tens or hundreds of thousands were killed.

Chapter 17

Faked versus Authentic Photographs: A World of Difference

Documentary photographs are powerful tools that are often used to bring an event to life or to prove that it actually took place. Therefore, the abuse or outright manufacture of such photographs is particularly reprehensible.

In pleading their case, those who believe (or who would have us believe) that a massacre was perpetrated in Nanking have made extensive use of photographs. When these so-called documentary photographs were first disseminated, they were immensely effective in swaying public opinion, convincing many people that the charges were accurate. However, when subjected to scrutiny, every one of these photographs was proven not only to have no connection with any event that took place in Nanking, but also to have been (1) faked or otherwise adulterated for propaganda purposes, (2) supplied with spurious captions, or (3) of unknown (and therefore, suspicious) provenance.

Iris Chang's *The Rape of Nanking* includes 12 pages of photographs. However, we can state with certainty that not a single one of them bears witness to a "Nanking Massacre." (See "*A Study of "The Rape of Nanking*" by Higashinakano Shudo and Fujioka Nobukatsu for a detailed treatment of this subject.)[123] In this chapter, we will show how they have been misrepresented, focusing on three photographs from Chang's book, which have also appeared in other books, as well as newspapers and magazines.

There is no dearth of photographs that portray the true situation in Nanking in late 1937 and thereafter. As I stated in Chapters 16, 120 Japanese newspaper reporters and photographers entered Nanking along with invading troops. The journalists were extremely diligent about gathering information and writing reports, which they wired to Japan nearly every day. As long as they didn't reveal any military secrets, they were free to cover whatever they liked. They explored every nook and cranny of Nanking, a rather small city, and took thousands of photographs. Those photographs were reproduced in hundreds of magazines and newspapers. Not one of them (even those that did not appear in the media) depicts a massacre. Postwar newspaper reporters, eager to prove that a massacre took place, have scoured photographic archives, looking for evidence. Their rummaging has been fruitless, which is not surprising, since none ever existed.

We have reproduced some of the photographs from four collections featured in the *Asahi Shinbun*, one of Japan's leading newspapers, during the month following the fall of Nanking on December 13, 1937 (on December 20, 22, 25, 30, and January 3). The newspaper also carried articles about Nanking under the Japanese occupation. It would be mistaken to construe these as propaganda photographs. They are genuine photographs taken by representatives of one of the dozen or so Japanese newspapers covering Nanking. Furthermore, they were published as soon as they were received, and were not altered in any way. These photographs present a true picture of life in Nanking at the time, and demonstrate that there was absolutely no basis for accusations of a massacre. (Unfortunately, they have been preserved only in reduced size, so they are not as clear as we would like. But they are authentic records of the situation in Nanking after the hostilities had ended.)

As we mentioned earlier, there are thousands of contemporaneous photographs that speak the truth about Nanking, which include those taken by individuals as well as journalists. Currently, we are in the process of assembling and cataloguing these photographs, which we hope to disseminate in the near future.

A. Faked or Misrepresented Photographs
in *The Rape of Nanking*

Example 1

This photograph has been reproduced in many publications (e.g., in the May 21, 1997 issue of *Newsweek*, Japan issue). However, it is a total fake — a composite created for propaganda purposes. The fakery is easy to detect if you look at the shadow cast by the man at the center brandishing a Japanese sword, and that cast by the soldier to his right. They are facing in different directions. Furthermore, the soldier with the sword is wearing a type of jacket never worn by Japanese soldiers. Any Japanese would be shocked to learn that this photograph had fooled the world's media.

Photograph 1

Example 2

The photographer's name and the site where the photograph 2 (next page) was taken are unknown, but we are certain that it has no connection with the Nanking Incident. This photograph has appeared in several books, eventually metamorphosing into evidence of the "Nanking Massacre." One of those books is *A Collection of Photographs of the Japanese Invasion of China* issued by the Xinhua Publishing Co. in 1984.

The photograph made its next appearance in 1997, in the second edition of a book edited by Shi Yong and bearing the same title as Chang's book, *The Rape of Nanking*, which also contains a photograph identical to this one (Photograph 2A). Its caption reads: "According to an article in the August 4, 1984 edition of the *Asahi Shinbun*, this is one of three photographs brought back to Japan by a former soldier who saw action in Nanking, and now resides in Miyazaki."[125]

However, the *Asahi Shinbun* article turned out to be totally erroneous. Another former soldier named Sato Susumu, a resident of Kanagawa Prefecture came forward and announced that he was in possession of a photograph identical to the one reproduced by the *Asahi Shinbun*. Mr. Sato joined the 19th Engineer Battalion at Huining, near the border between North Korea and China, in October 1931, and was assigned to guard duty at the border. Toward the end of that year, he bought 10 photographs, all similar in nature, which were being sold as souvenirs at a combination stationery store and photographer's studio in Huining. One of them was the photograph in question. The caption on the photograph purchased by Mr. Sato reads "Heads of Bandits Shot to Death in Tieling" (Manchuria). The bandits were shot and subsequently decapitated by the soldiers of Zhang Xueliang (1898-), Manchurian warlord and, for a time, Nationalist government chief in Manchuria.

Photograph 2B (which appears both in *A Collection of Photographs of the Japanese Invasion of China* and Shi Yong's *The Rape of Nanking*, and which is identical to another of the 10

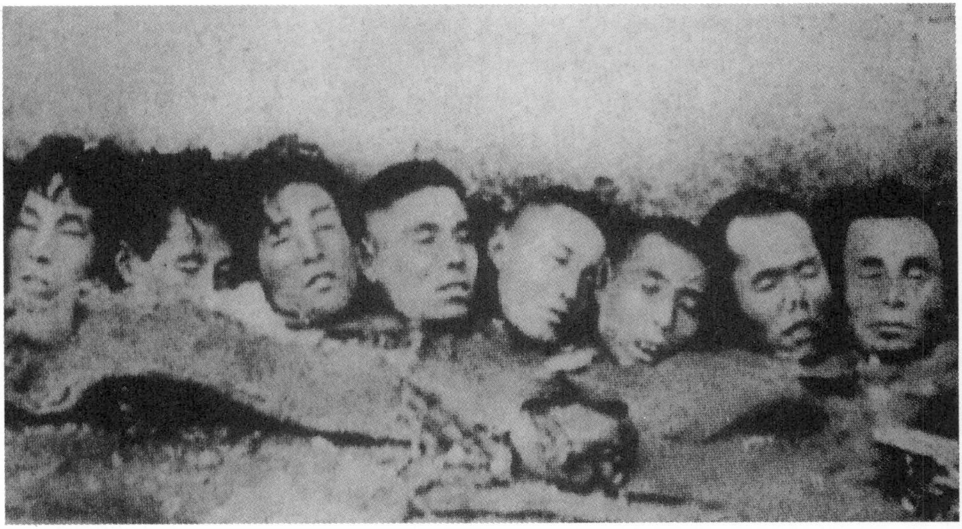
Photograph 2

Photograph 2A

owned by Mr. Sato) shows soldiers using a large hay cutter to sever a man's head. The soldiers are wearing Nationalist uniforms, so they are Chinese, not Japanese. The *Asahi Shinbun*, realizing its error, printed an apology in which it retracted the August 4 article in its entirety.

However, *A Collection of Photographs of the Japanese Invasion of China* maintains that the heads in this same photograph are those of Chinese murdered while defending their nation against the Japanese. Its authors have miraculously transformed bandits executed by Nationalist soldiers into Chinese massacred by Japanese troops. In *The Rape of Nanking*, Shi Yong, inspired by the erroneous article in the *Asahi Shinbun*, claims that the severed heads are presented as victims of the conflict in Nanking. Going a step further, Iris Chang asserts that this photograph constitutes proof of the "Nanking Massacre." This is another example of the depraved methods used to concoct "evidence."

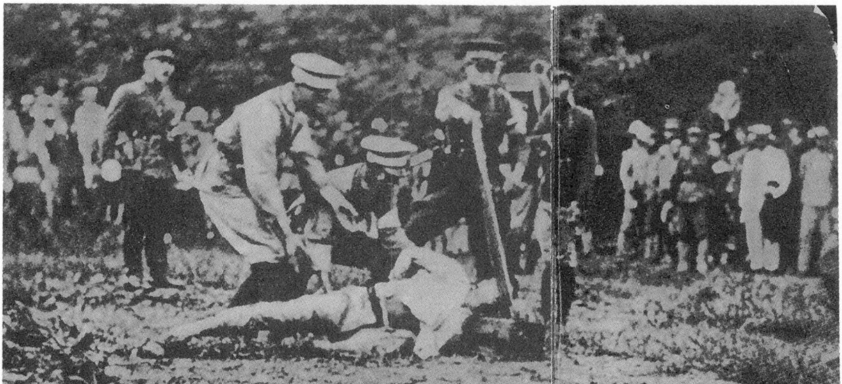

Photograph 2B

Example 3

The provenance of this photograph has been ascertained. It was taken by former soldier Murase Moriyasu. The version that appears in Chang's book has obviously been trimmed, for reasons that are not clear to us (Photograph 3A is the original). Murase took this panoramic photograph at the juncture of the Yangtze and Jia rivers. Takahashi Yoshihiko (former major and head of an observation party attached to the Headquarters of the 2nd Independent Mountain Artillery Regiment), who took part in a conflict on the upper reaches of the Yangtze at Xinhezhen, was kind

Photograph 3

enough to provide an explanation. At about 6:00 a.m. on December 14, 1937, Takahashi's unit encountered a large group of enemy soldiers who had fled Nanking through Yijiang Gate, at Xinhezhen. An intense battle ensued. Though greatly outnumbered, the Japanese persevered and finally, at about 11:00 a.m., prevailed. Their opponents began jumping into the river. The Japanese fired at them from the bank, killing most of them. Their corpses were carried by the current to the confluence of the Yangtze and Jia rivers, where this photograph was taken. Since most of the bodies are facing in the same direction, it is obvious that, carried by the current, they drifted downstream, clustering as they neared the riverbank.

This is, without a doubt, a ghastly scene. However, these men were combatants who were killed during a war. They cannot rightly be called massacre victims, as we argued in Chapter 1. What are we to make of a nation that attempts to gain the sympathy of the international community by complaining that its war dead were victims of a massacre?

Photograph 3A

B. Authentic Photographs Portraying Life in Nanking After the Conflict

Asahi Shinbun Feature No. 1: December 20, 1937

Title: "Peace Returns to Nanking: Joyful Residents of Nanking Welcome the Imperial Army"

Photographed by *Asahi Shinbun* correspondent Kawamura on December 17.

1: "Soldiers Enjoy Shopping in Nanking"(By the fifth day of the occupation, outdoor stalls had cropped up all over the city. Note that the soldiers are unarmed.)

2: "Now that the Imperial Army has entered Nanking, farmers can tend their fields outside the city in safety"

3: "A group of returning refugees escorted by the Imperial Army"(With peace restored, residents who had evacuated to areas outside the city, felt that it was safe to return to their homes, and streamed back into the city. See Chapter 3, p. 19.)

4: "An open-air barbershop in a peaceful city" (Open-air barbershops have long been a common sight in China. In this photograph, smiling adults and children are wearing homemade armbands depicting the Japanese flag. By the fifth day of the occupation, street vendors selling all sorts of wares were open for business, and soldiers strolled around the Safety Zone without their weapons.)

Asahi Shinbun Feature No. 2: December 22, 1937

Title: “Yesterday’s Enemy Is Today’s Friend: Japanese Acts of Kindness”

Photographed by *Asahi Shinbun* correspondent Kawamura.

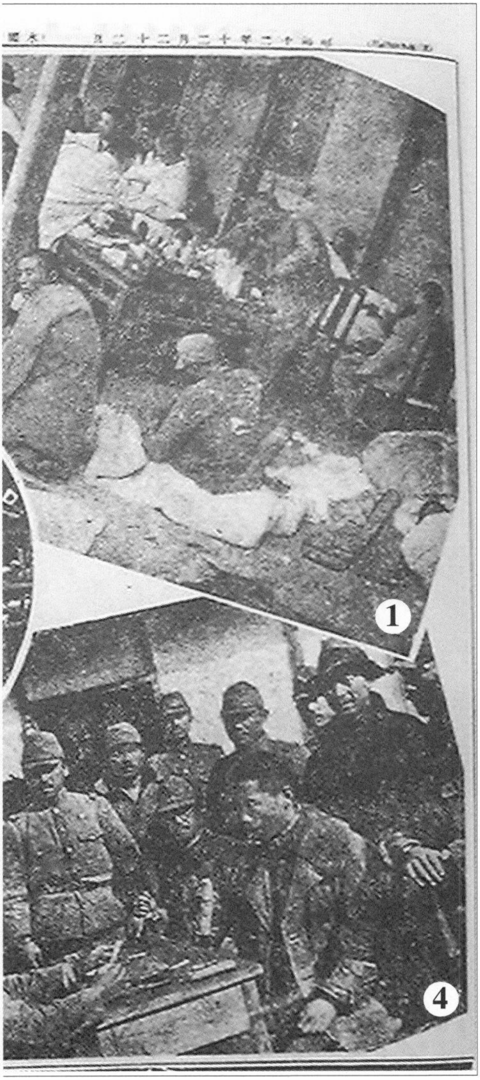

1: "Wounded Chinese soldiers receiving medical treatment" (Wounded members of the Nanking Defense Corps, abandoned by their commander, Tang Shengzhi, are treated by a Japanese army physician and a member of the medical corps.)
2: "Hungry prisoners of war are fed by Imperial Army soldiers" (Compliant prisoners were treated kindly.)
3: "With the guns of war now silent, good will reigns in Nanking"
4: "Training Unit Staff Officer Maj. Shen Boshi chats with the commander of the Tayama Unit" (The Training Unit was the Chinese Army's elite division. Later, Maj. Shen later served in Wang Jingwei's administration.)
5: "Friendships Blossom in Nanking"

Asahi Shinbun Feature No. 3: December 25, 1937
Title: "Nanking Smiles: City Sketches"

Photographed by *Asahi Shinbun* correspondent Hayashi.

1: "Children playing with toy tanks — Japanese soldiers join in the fun (on Zhongshan Road, Nanking)"
2: "Now that the war has ended, neighborhood children use a broken carriage as a playhouse (in a residential area of Nanking)"
3: "The kindness of members of the Imperial Army's Medical Corps deepens Sino-Japanese friendship (in the Refugee Zone)"
4: "Hymns in praise of peace resound from a church garden (on Ninghai Road, Nanking)" (John Magee was the pastor of this church — the Episcopal Church of Nanking. The photographs he took were later used as evidence of a massacre, but the subjects of most of them are persons wounded in the war. Rev. Magee was a witness for the prosecution at the IMTFE, where he testified for two full days, enumerating several hundred Japanese atrocities. However, when he was cross-examined by defense attorneys, he conceded that he had personally witnessed only one murder. Pressed to elaborate, Magee said that he had seen Japanese soldiers kill a straggler who was trying to escape. But in his diary, he reveals that he had perjured himself — he writes that he had not witnessed the murder. This photograph exposes the huge difference between his claims of Japanese atrocities and the truth.)

兵隊さんは子供と遊ぶ

Asahi Shinbun Feature No. 4: December 30, 1937

Title: "Sino-Japanese Friendship Deepens as Nanking Prepares to Greet the New Year"

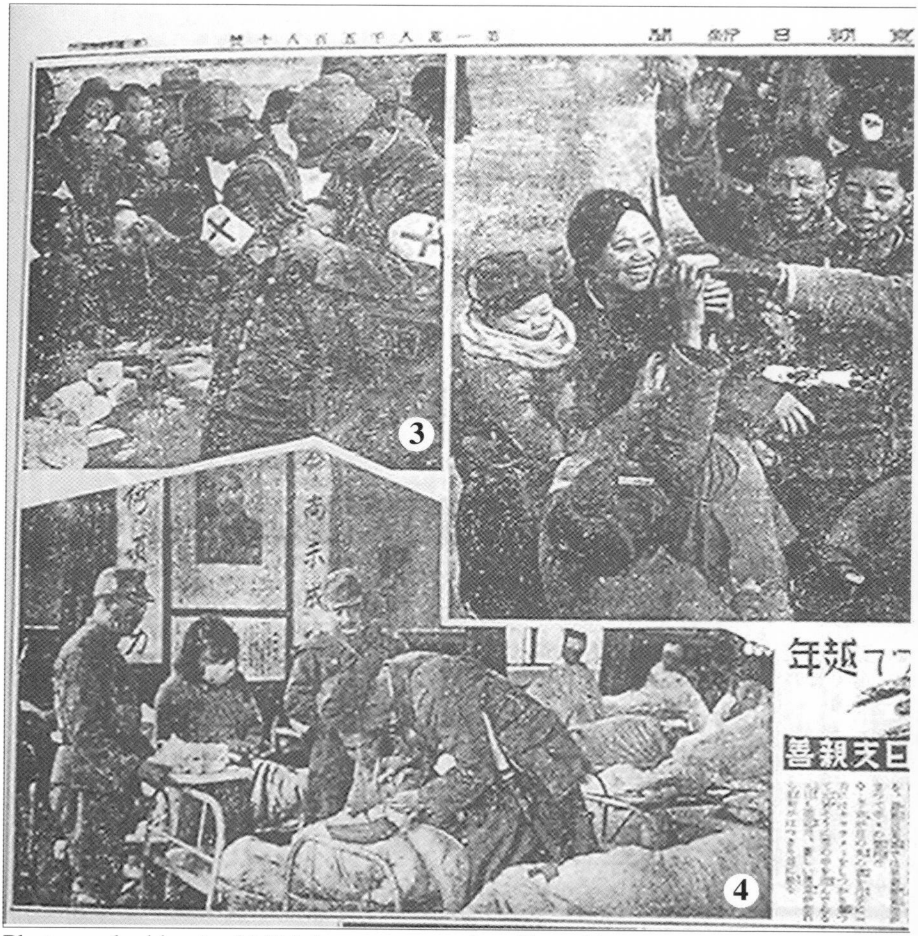

Photographed by *Asahi Shinbun* correspondent Hayashi.

1: "Chinese shoemaker offers to repair soldiers' boots for the New Year."
2: "A grateful mother receives milk for her child from a kind Japanese officer"
3: "The Medical Corps in action: Comforting a little boy as he is treated for trachoma"
4: "A Medical Department in action: Changing a dressing" (This feature is accompanied by an article entitled "Nanking Anticipates the Arrival of the New Year, Complete With Rice Cakes.")

Memorial Services Held for Chinese Soldiers Killed in Action

The photographs shown above were taken at a memorial service for Chinese soldiers killed in action. The service took place on February 8, 1938 under the auspices of Japanese military authorities and the Nanking Self-Government Committee at a cemetery near Yijiang Gate. Both Japanese and Chinese priests officiated. Col. Uemura Toshimichi, chief of staff of the Shanghai Expeditionary Force, wrote the following account of the service in his war journal on that same day.

> We held a memorial service for Chinese soldiers at Yijiang Gate. They were our enemies, but offerings of flowers to one's fallen enemy is a demonstration of compassion, which is an integral part of bushido. Members of the Self-Government Committee, as well as Japanese and Chinese priests, were in attendance.[126]

The photograph shown below was taken on February 28, 1938, the date on which another memorial service, arranged by Lt.-Gen. Fujita, commander of the 3rd Division, was held at the same site. Otani Koyo, head priest of Higashi Hongan Temple in Kyoto, officiated.

These photographs are contemporaneous records, and they prove that Japanese military personnel adhered to the *bushido* code by praying for the repose of the souls of the enemy dead. They should also negate the evil demagoguery that led the world to believe that Japanese soldiers murdered Chinese indiscriminately or orchestrated a holocaust.

Source: *Illustrated Weekly*, No. 27 (February 8, 1938) issued by the Cabinet Information Office

Source: *The Second Sino-Japanese War: An Illustrated Report*, March 1938 (Osaka Mainichi Shinbunsha)

Notes

1. The "Outline of Measures Towards Jewish Peoples" was adopted during theKonoe administration on the basis of a decision made at a meeting of five senior ministers on December 6, 1938. It reads as follows.

The maintenance of close, amicable relations with Germany and Italy is axial to Imperial Japan's foreign policy. Consequently, the welcoming of the Jewish people into the Empire must, in principle, be avoided in light of the exclusionist policy adopted toward the Jews by our allies.

However, an exclusionary stance as extreme as that taken by Germany is simply incompatible with the spirit of racial equality that we have advocated for so many years.

Furthermore, such a stance would be extremely disadvantageous to the Empire, given the present state of emergency it faces. We must introduce foreign capital so that we may accomplish the economic construction needed to wage war, and we must not allow relations with the United States to deteriorate. For the aforementioned reasons, the following policy shall be adopted toward the Jewish people.

Policy

1. Jews who are presently residing in Japan, Manchukuo [Manchuria], and China shall be treated in the same fair manner as are other foreign nationals; no measures shall be implemented that discriminate against them in any particular way.
2. Newly arrived Jews in Japan, Manchukuo and China shall be treated fairly within the scope of general rules governing the entry of foreign nationals.
3. The invitation of Jews to Japan, Manchukuo and China shall be avoided. However, exceptions shall be made for those persons possessing special attributes that may prove useful, e.g., capitalists and technical experts.

2. Between July and September, 1939, Sugihara Chiune, Japanese consul-general in Kaunas (Kovno), Lithuania, issued thousands of visas to desperate Jews. By doing so, he saved more than 6,000 lives. It is often said that in issuing those visas, Sugihara defied instructions from the Japanese government. However, if that had been the case, persons holding them would have been denied entry to Japan. For further information, see Hillel Levine, *In Search of Sugihara* (New York: Free Press, 1996).

Lt.-Gen. Higuchi Kiichiro, head of the Harbin Special Agency, lent his support to the first conference of the Jewish communities in the Far East held at Harbin in 1937. Later, he aided many Jews who had fled to Manchuria. His good deeds have been recorded in Israelis Golden Book (Register No. 4026).

Colonel Yasue Senko, head of the Dalian Special Agency, also assisted Jews who escaped to Manchuria in 1938. Subsequently, he made a special effort to protect Jewish communities in Manchuria and Shanghai. His contributions are also recorded in the Golden Book (Register No. 4028).

3. Indian legal scholar (1886-1967) who served as one of the justices at the Tokyo Trials. Justice Pal submitted a dissenting opinions on the grounds that retroactive application of the law was illegal.

4. Published as *Paaru Hakase no Nippon Muzairon* (Tokyo:

Keibunsha, 1963).

5. Published as *Tokyo Saiban to wa nani ka* (Tokyo: Nihon Kogyo Shinbunsha, 1983).

6. Published as *Nankin gyakusatsu no kyoko* (Tokyo: Nihon Kyobunsha, 1984).

7. Published as *Matsui Taisho no jinchu nikki* (Tokyo: Fuyo Shobo, 1985). Researcher Itakura Yoshiaki wrote an article indicating that I had misread portions of Gen. Matsui's handwritten diary, which appeared in the Winter 1985 issue of *Rekishi to jinbutsu* (History and Personalities), published by Chuo Koronsha. This article inspired a piece entitled "Tanaka Masaaki Tampers With Gen. Matsui's Diary," which ran in the November 24 and 25, 1985 editions of the *Asahi Shinbun*. Honda Katsuichi was one of the writers of the article, which can only be construed as an underhanded means of exacting revenge for my having pointed out the gross inaccuracies in his articles about the Nanking Incident, serialized in the same newspaper. I sent a letter objecting to the campaign to brand me as a falsifier of history to the *Asahi Shinbun*, but it was never printed. It is true that I misread some portions of the diary (which was extremely difficult to decipher), but this was an error on my part, not an attempt to misrepresent Gen. Matsui, which would have been pointless. For full details, see "Honda shi! Nanji koso Nankin jiken no kaizan joshuhan" (Honda Is a Habitual Falsifier of the Nanking Incident) in *Getsuyo Hyoron*, No. 834 , written by Itakura, who originally discovered the errors.

8. Published as *Nankin jiken no sokatsu* (Tokyo: Kenkosha, 1987).

9. The figure stated in the judgement against General Matsui Iwane.

10. Harold Timperley, ed., *What War Means: Japanese Terror in China* (1938) (New York: Books for Library Press, 1969).

11. Hsü Shuhsi, ed. *Documents of the Nanking Safety Zone* (Shanghai: Kelly & Walsh, 1939) p. 17 (December 17, 1937);

pp. 18, 20 (December 18, 1937); p. 48 (December 21, 1937); p. 57 (December 27, 1937).

12. *Frankfurter Zeitung*, December 19, 1937.

13. Tanaka Masaaki, ed., *Matsui Iwane Taisho no jinchu nikki* (War Journal of General Matsui Iwane (Tokyo: Fuyo Shobo, 1985), p. 134.

14. Hora Tomio, *Nankin daigyakusatsu no shomei* (Proof of the Great Nanking Massacre) (Tokyo: Asahi Shinbunsha, 1987), p. 179.

15. City of Nanking Historical Document Research Association, *Shogen: Nankin daigyakusatsu* (Testimonies: The Great Nanking Massacre), trans., Himeda Mitsuyoshi and Kagami Mitsuyuki (Tokyo: Aoki Shoten, 1984), p. 178.

16. Iris Chang, *The Rape of Nanking: The Forgotten Holocaust of World War II* (New York: Penguin Books, 1998), p. 139.

17. Hsü, *op. cit.*, pp. 14-15.

18. IMTFE (International Military Tribunal for the Far East), *Proceedings*, Court Reporteris Transcript, August 29, 1946, p. 4,551.

19. *Ibid.*, February 18, 1948, p. 40,027.

20. Hsü, *op. cit.*, p. 84.

21. Lewis C.S. Smythe, *War Damage in the Nanking Area, December 1937 to March 1938: Urban and Rural Surveys, On Behalf of the Nanking International Relief Committee* (Shanghai: Mercury Press, 1938).

22. *Ibid.*

23. *Ibid.*

24. Tanaka, *op. cit.*, p. 135.

25. IMTFE, *op. cit.*, Court Reporter's Transcript, July 26, 1946, No. 35.

26. *Ibid.*, July 29, 1946, No. 36.

27. *Tokyo Nichinichi Shinbun*, December 26, 1937.

28. Nankin Senshi Henshu Iinkai (Battle of Nanking Editorial Committee), *Nankin senshi* (The Battle of Nanking), vol. 6 (Tokyo: Kaikosha, 1993).

29. Nankin Senshi Henshu Iinkai, *op. cit.*, vol. 7.
30. Nankin Senshi Henshu Iinkai, *op. cit.*, vol. 6.
31. See Guo Moruo, *Konichisen kaisoroku* (Reflections on the War Against Japan), trans. Okazaki Toshio (Tokyo: Chuo Koronsha, 1959). According to Guo, the Nationalist Party's Political Bureau, headed by Kang Ze (Zhou Enlai and Huang Qixiang were its deputy chairmen) established three departments whose responsibilities were to disseminate anti-Japanese propaganda and gather information. Kang Ze was head of the special detachment that collected massive amounts of data in Nanking.
32. Timperley, *op. cit.*
33. Ishii Itaro, *Gaikokan no issho* (A Diplomatic Career) (Tokyo: Yomiuri Shinbunsha, 1980), p. 305-306.
34. *Ibid.*, p. 300.
35. *Ibid.*, p. 303.
36. *Ibid.*, p. 459.
37. *Ibid.*, p. 460.
38. Fujiwara Akira, *Nankin daigyakusatsu* (The Great Nanking Massacre) (Tokyo: Iwanami Booklet, 1992.
39. Guo Qi, *Lamenting the Fall of Our Capital* ([Original publication date]; reprinted as The *Nanking Massacre*, Taipei: Zhongwai Tushu Chubanshe, 1978); reproduced in Nankin Jiken Chosa Kenkyukai Hen (Nanking Incident Research Group), *Chugoku Kankei Shiryo Hen* (Chinese References), vol. 2 of *Nankin Jiken Shiryoshu* (Nanking Incident Source Material) (Tokyo: Aoki Shoten, 1992), p. 234.
40. IMTFE, *op. cit.*, Court Reporter's Transcript, December 6, 1957, No. 309.
41. Hsü, *op. cit.*
42. In a letter to the Japanese Embassy dated December 17, 1937, John Rabe wrote, "On the 13th when your troops entered the city, we had nearly all the civilian population gathered in a Zone." Hsü Shu-Hsi, ed., *Documents of the Nanking Safety Zone* (Shanghai: Kelly & Walsh, 1939), pp. 14-15.

43. IMTFE, *op. cit.*, Exhibit No. 323 (excerpt from Prosecution Exhibit No. 1744), Court Reporter's Transcript, No. 210, read by defense attorney.
44. *Ibid.*, Testimony of James McCallum, Exhibit No. 309.
45. Lewis S.C. Smythe, War Damage in the Nanking Area, December 1937 to March 1938: Urban and Rural Surveys, On Behalf of the Nanking International Relief Committee (Nanking: Nanking International Relief Committee, June 1938).
46. Domei Tsushin (Federated News Agency), founded in 1936, was Japan's official news service until 1945.
47. *Sekai to Nippon* (Japan and the World), No. 413, 05 April 1959.
48. Fujiwara, *op. cit.*, pp. 28-29.
49. Infantry School, "Disposition of Prisoners of War" in *A Study of Combat Methods Used Against Chinese Troops* (Tokyo, January 1933).
50. Convention (IV) Respecting the Laws and Customs of War on Land and Its Annex: Regulations Concerning the Laws and Customs of War on Land (The Hague, 18 October 1907).
51. Shinobu Junpei, *Shanghai sen to kokusai ho* (The Conflict at Shanghai and International Law) (Tokyo: Maruzen, 1932), p. 125.
52. Tabata Shigejiro, *Kokusai ho shinko*, (International Law: Revised Edition) (Tokyo: Toshindo, 1991), vol. 2, p. 203.
53. Paul Carell and Günter Böddecker, *Die Gefangenen: Leben und Überleben deutschen Soldaten hinter Stacheldraht* (The Prisoners: The Lives and Survival of German Soldiers Behind Barbed Wire) (Frankfurt am Main: Ullstein, 1980).
54. Hora, *op. cit.*, p. 304.
55. Ara Ken'ichi, "Japanese Witnesses to the Fall of Nanking," *Seiron*, May 1986.
56. IMTFE, *op. cit.*, Court Reporter's Transcript, November 11, 1947, No. 310.
57. Masui Koichi, *Kankan saibanshi* (Trials of Chinese Who

Collaborated With the Japanese) (Tokyo: Misuzu Shobo, 1977), p. 110.

58. Honda Katsuichi, *Nankin e no Michi* (The Road to Nanking) (Asahi Shinbunsha, 1987) (Paperback: Asahi Bunko, 1994).

59. Suzuki Akira, *Nankin daigyakusatsu no maboroshi* (The Illusion of a Great Nanking Massacre) (Tokyo: Bungei Shunju, 1982), pp. 189-197.

60. Boei Kenshujo Senshishitsu (Defense Research Institute, Military History Department), *Senshi Sosho: Shina Jihen Rikugun Sakusen (1)* (Military History Series: Army Operations During the Second Sino-Japanese War, Part 1) (Tokyo: Asagumo Shinbunsha, 1976).

61. Honda Katsuichi, "Nankin e no michi" (The Road to Nanking) in *Asahi Journal* 21 and 22, 07 September and 14 September 1984.

62. Estimates of the number of prisoners killed during the skirmish vary (Kurihara, 5,000-6,000; Sgt. Hoshi Shunzo, 2,000; and Maj.-Gen. Hirabayashi, 1,000-3,000). These differences are understandable, given the circumstances.

63. The shooting of prisoners who attempt to escape or who are insubordinate is sanctioned by international law.

64. Committee for the Investigation of Japanese War Crimes Committed in Nanking: Procurator of the District Court, Nanking, *Summary Report on the Investigation of Japanese War Crimes Committed in Nanking* (IMTFE Document No. 1706, p. 2).

65. *Ibid.*

66. *Ibid.*

67. *Ibid.*, p. 3.

68. IMTFE, *op. cit.*, November 11, 1948, vol. 2, p. 103.

69. City of Nanking Historical Document Research Association, *op. cit.*, p. 167.

70. For details, see *Sankei Shinbun*, 10 August 1985; Ara Ken'ichi, "Kaku datta Nankin daigyakusatsu no shoko" (Proof That the Nanking Massacre Was Invented) in *Seiron* (Tokyo: Sankei

Shinbunsha, October 1985).

71. Compiled by the City of Nanking Government Secretariat, March 1939.

72. Ichiki Yoshimichi, ed. *Nankin* (Nanking). Nankin Nippon Shoko Kaigisho (Nanking Japanese Chamber of Commerce), 1941.

73. Hora, *op. cit.*, p. 201.

74. City of Nanking Historical Document Research Association, *op. cit.*, p. 171.

75. Hora Tomio, ed., *Nankin Jiken I* (The Nanking Incident: Part I), Nicchu senso shiryo (References from the Sino-Japanese Wars), vol. 8 (Tokyo: Kawade Shobo Shinsha, 1973), p. 389.

76. *Tokyo Nichinichi Shimbun*, November 25, 1937.

77. Smythe, *op. cit.*, p. 7.

78. *Ibid.*, p. 8.

79. Hora Tomio, *Ketteiban: Nankin daigyakusatsu* (The Authoritative Version of the Great Nanking Massacre). (Tokyo: Tokuma Shoten, 1987), p. 155.

80. *Ibid.*

81. IMTFE, *op. cit.*, Court Reporter's Transcript, August 29, 1946, No. 58.

82. He Yingqin, *Modern Chinese History: The Conflict With Japan*, ed. Wu Xiangxiang (Taipei: Wenxing Shudian, 1948), p. 82.

83. Sankei Shinbun, *The Secret Memoirs of Chiang Kai-Shek* (Tokyo: Sankei Shinbun, 1976), vol. 12, p. 69.

84. See article by Takagi Keizo in *Getsuyo Hyoron* (Monday Review), 27 February 1984.

85. Agnes Smedley, *Battle Hymn of China* (1944; reprint, New York: DaCapo Press, 1975).

86. Nanking City Historical Document Research Committee, *op. cit.*, p. 218.

87. Research Committee on Current Affairs, *Chinese Military Affairs in Wartime*, *China in Wartime* (Yan'an, 1941), p. 219.

88. Nanking City Historical Document Research Committee, *op. cit.*, p. 217.

89. *Ibid*., p. 162.
90. *Ibid*., p. 60.
91. Nationalist government foreign minister.
92. Harold Timperley, ed., *Gaikokujin no mita Nihongun no boko* (Acts of Violence Committed by Japanese Military Personnel as Witnessed by Foreign Nationals) (Tokyo: Hyodensha, 1982); originally published as *What War Means: Japanese Terror in China* (1938) (New York: Books for Library Press, 1969).
93. Fujiwara Akira, *op. cit*., p. 9.
94. *Ibid*., p. 9; Matsumoto Shigeharu, *Shanhai jidai* (Shanghai Sojourn) (Tokyo: Chuko Shinsho, 1975), vol. 2, p. 250.
95. Matsumoto, *op. cit*., pp. 249-250.
96. *Ibid*., p. 250.
97. Suzuki Akira, *Shin Nankin daigyakusatsu no maboroshi* (The Illusion of a Great Nanking Massacre: Updated Edition) (Tokyo: Asuka Shinsha, June 1999).
98. Modern Research Institute, Chinese Academy of Social Sciences, *Notable Foreign Visitors to China: The Modern Era* (n.p.: Zhongguo Shehui Chubanshe (China Social Sciences Publishing Co.), December 1981).
99. Matsumoto, *op. cit*., p. 251.
100. See article in *Sekai to Nippon* (Japan and the World), n.d., pp. 447-449.
101. F. Tillman Durdin, "Japanese Atrocities Marked Fall of Nanking After Chinese Command Fled," *New York Times*, 09 January 1938.
102. *Ibid*.
103. Fujiwara, *op. cit*., p. 6.
104. "Ex-Chinese Officers Among U.S. Refugees: Colonel and His Aides Admit Blaming the Japanese for Crimes in Nanking," *New York Times*, 04 January 1938.
105. Durdin, *op. cit*.
106. McDonald, *The London Times*, 18 December 1937.
107. "War in China," *Time*, 27 December 1937, p. 13.

108. "War in China," *Time*, 14 February 1938, p. 17.
109. Ministry of the Interior, *Shuppan keisatsu ho* (Publishing Supervision Law Bulletin), No. 110, p. 226.
110. *Ibid.*; this information was provided by Ara Ken'ichi.
111. Former name of *Mainichi Shinbun.*
112. *Sekai Nippo* (World Daily Report), 01 September 1982.
113. Goto Kosaku. *The Truth About the Battle of Nanking: The Story of the 6th Division.* (Kumamoto Nichinichi Shinbunsha, April 1966).
114. *Sekai to Nippon* (Japan and the World), August 31, 1957.
115. *Ibid.*, p. 14.
116. Honda Katsuichi, *op. cit.*, pp. 41-42.
117. Liberal Democratic Party.
118. An iconoclastic critic and acute observer of social trends, Oya (1900-1970) was awarded the Kikuchi Kan literary prize for *Honoo* wa nagareru (Flames Flow).
119. Saijo (1892-1970) was a poet and educator who is perhaps best known for the many song lyrics he wrote. During a sojourn in France, he was befriended by symbolist poet Paul ValEry. Representative of his poetry is the anthology *Roningyo* (Wax doll).
120. A poet known for his use of colloquial language, Kusano (1903-88) studied in China. His best-known work is *Teihon kaeru* (Frog Poems), which portray the human condition from the viewpoint of a frog.
121. One of Japan's most highly regarded woman novelists known for her realistic depictions of urban working-class life, Hayashi (1903-51) is best known for her first novel, *Horo ki* (Journal of a vagabond), based on her travels in Japan and abroad.
122. A literary critic whose writings span a wide range of cultures and genres, Kobayashi (1902-83) was a prolific author whose works include a critical biography of Dostoevsky.
123. Fujioka Nobukatsu and Higashinakano Shudo, "*The Rape of Nanking*" *no kenkyu* (A Study on *The Rape of Nanking*) (Tokyo: Shodensha, 1999).

124. Photography Department, Xinhua News Agency, *Riben qinhua tupian shiliaoji* (A Collection of Photographs of the Japanese Invasion of China) (Beijing: Xinhua Publishing Co., 1984), p. 90.

125. Shi Yong, ed., *The Rape of Nanking: Undeniable History in Photographs* (Chicago: Innovative Publishing Group, 1997), p.113.

126. Nankin Senshi Henshu Iinkai Hen (Battle of Nanking Editorial Committee), *Nankin Senshi Shiryoshu* (Source Material Relating to the Battle of Nanking) (Tokyo: Kaikosha, 1993), p. 299.

127. The name derives from the last speech given by Sun Yatsen in Japan, in 1924.

Index

About the Author

Tanaka Masaaki was born in 1911 in Nagano Prefecture. In 1933, after graduating from the Academy of Asian Studies, he was hired by the Dai Ajia Kyokai (Pan-Asian Association).[127] Mr. Tanaka organized the Seinen Ajia Domei (Youth Alliance for Asia), an organization whose membership included Indonesians and Indians as well as Japanese, in 1934, and took part in its campaigns to win independence for the nations of Asia. In 1936, he accompanied Army General Matsui Iwane, the Association's chairman, on an inspection tour of China, and met with Chiang Kai-shek and other eminent Chinese. When the Association was absorbed into the Dai Nippon Koa Domei (Japan Pan-Asian Alliance) in 1941, he remained on its staff.

Mr. Tanaka was drafted into the Army in December 1942, and assigned to the Central China Field Ordnance Depot in Shanghai as a cryptographer.

He returned to Japan in 1946, and accepted a position as editor-in-chief of the *Nanshin Jiji Shinbun*. Forced to resign from the newspaper during one of the purges launched by Occupation authorities, he moved to Tokyo and went to work for the Nippon Seisan Kyoiku Kyokai (Association for Increased Productivity Through Education). In 1952, Mr. Tanaka published *Justice Radhabinod Pal Absolves Japan*. In 1958, he joined the Sekai

Renpo Kensetsu Domei (United World Federalists of Japan) as secretary-general, a position he held for 15 years.

Since then, he has served as managing director of the Kokusai Heiwa Kyokai (International Peace Association), and as a lecturer at Takushoku University. Through his work as a critic, he has endeavored to disseminate Dr. Pal's judgement in Japan's favor, to publicize the truth about the conflict in and subsequent occupation of Nanking, to achieve independence for the nations of Asia, and to dispel the masochistic perception of history now prevalent in Japan. Among his many writings are *Justice Radhabinod Pal Absolves Japan. Later, The Truth About the Tokyo Trials, The Fabrication of the Nanking Massacre, The War Journal of General Matsui Iwane, What Really Happened in Nanking: The Refutation of a Common Myth, A 20-Year History of the United World Federalist Movement, The United World Federalist Movement in Thought and Action, The Truth About the Tokyo Trials, The Fabrication of the Nanking Massacre*, and *Sun Yatsen's Quest for Sino-Japanese Harmony and Wang Jingwei.*